ERIC & ERNIE

ERIC & ERNIE

The autobiography of
Morecambe & Wise

Referee:
Dennis Holman

W. H. Allen
London and New York
A division of Howard & Wyndham Ltd
1973

© *Eric Morecambe, Ernie Wise & Dennis Holman 1973*

*This book or parts thereof may not be
reproduced without permission in writing.*

*First published September 1973
Reprinted before publication*

*Printed and bound in Great Britain by
Butler and Tanner Ltd, Frome and London,
for the publishers W. H. Allen & Co. Ltd,
44 Hill Street, W1X 8LB*

ISBN O 491 01211 X

PART ONE
Starters

1

The boys had hit a snag. They had been asked to write a book and were arguing about who should hold the pen. There were obvious advantages for the one who wielded this mightier thing than the sword. He could steal every scene—by inflection, innuendo, by being arch or patronising, or even excessively modest. Even, as Eric indignantly pointed out, by using semi-colons.

'As for exclamation marks,' and he levelled a finger at Ernie, 'he has been known to use as many as eight in a row, and even I know five is the limit.'

'All right, no exclamation marks,' Ernie conceded.

'Definitely, no exclamation marks.'

At one stage they were seriously considering holding the pen together, when a further issue looked like bogging them down in yet another series of marathon talks. Whose hand would be nearer the ballpoint?

At this point I arrived on the scene, and it was agreed that I should referee the contest to see justice done.

Has it been done? Was it a fair fight? Well, at least no holds have been barred. I have pried and I have probed. I have opened cupboards and found some pretty hoary skeletons. I have seen bosoms bared, raw nerves exposed and fangs unsheathed from behind forced smiles. Where facts have been in dispute, parents, wives, relatives, friends, rivals, colleagues and customers have been called in like linesmen at a football match to help adjudicate.

3

My first problem in refereeing this autobiographical duel was to decide who in fairness should be allowed to begin the tale. There are five months and sixteen days between Ernie, a Sagittarian, who said hello to the world on 27 November 1925, and Eric, who uttered his first squawk on 14 May 1926, under the sign of Taurus the Bull—which Ernie claims was appropriate enough.

The decision could have been a tricky one. But Ernie suddenly conceded that his partner could have the first word provided that he, Ernie, reserved the right to the last. This was agreed.

Let me set the scene: a cinema in Manchester where Eric is to be auditioned by the well-known band leader and impresario, Jack Hylton. Hylton is sitting in the auditorium with twenty-five of his musicians and by his side his thirteen-year-old protégé, Ernie Wise. It is August 1939.

ERIC   The excitement had begun the day before with a long-awaited telegram from Jack Hylton, telling me I was to collect the first prize for a talent competition I had won three months before at Hoylake, a resort on the coast near Liverpool. The prize?

Not in money or kind or even book token. But in opportunity —an audition before the great Jack Hylton himself. The discoveries show he was presenting was in constant need of fresh talent, and between them he and Bryan Michie had to find it. At the time I felt my prize was a complete swizz. A boy of thirteen likes to win something tangible, something he can eat, or show his chums, or even hock, especially when he has competed, as I had, virtually under duress.

Sadie, my wise and ambitious mum, certainly thought otherwise. She had been drumming it into my head all the way over from our home in Morecambe, on the Lancashire coast, that, who knows, this day might affect my whole life. She was right, of course. Looking up at me from the auditorium was the smug mug of Ernie Wise, his beady eyes immediately spotting a hot property.

ERNIE   So hot, I had to nudge Jack Hylton to keep him awake. The mother's eyes were beamed on us like lasers. I had to see

4

that the kid got his prize, though the act looked like developing into a filibuster.

ERIC Referee, please rule him out of order.

ERNIE On what grounds?

ERIC Flippant, impertinent and, if you can spell it, irrelevant interruption.

(Ernie is ruled out of order)

ERIC I had six pieces in my repertoire, including a comedy number, originally sung by Ella Shields, called *I'm Not All There*. I had to look gormless which was difficult. . . .

ERNIE *Difficult?*

ERIC Yes, *difficult*—without a comedy outfit, a cut-down tail-coat held together by an enormous safety-pin, short evening dress trousers, black shoes, red socks held up by purple suspenders, a bootlace for a tie, a large piece of check tablecloth for a pocket handkerchief, a beret flat on my head, a kiss curl over one eye, large spectacle frames and an outsize sixpenny lollypop which was the only perk I ever got out of this act.

ERNIE Some 'perk'. We had to watch him licking it. Nauseating.

ERIC My props were in a suitcase. I remember my mother adding a few finishing touches, then saying, 'Now go out there and give them all you've got. Make the words clear. If you pull it off I'll buy you an airgun.'

I had knocked them out at Hoylake, but all I got from Jack Hylton was, 'OK, what else?'

ERNIE He had so many relatives falling about out of politeness, he thought he was the bee's knees.

ERIC Referee, shut him up or send him off.

(Ernie was shut up)

ERIC My *pièce de résistance* was an impression of Bud Flanagan in a big racoon coat and a battered straw hat singing *Underneath the Arches* and *Down and Out Blues*. Then came my Fred Astaire impression in top hat and tails. Finally I blacked up for my impression of G. H. Elliott, 'the chocolate-coloured coon'.

There was scattered applause with a little clap from the protégé.

One of the musicians, I heard later, had remarked to him 'You'd better watch out. This lad is good. He's going to be in the show.'

This patter of hands was the prize. What a let-down after the heady excitement of the finals at Hoylake with that wonderful sense of secret gloating over hated rivals you had beaten. I remember my mother going down from the stage by the side of the pit with its huge cinema organ. She approached the great man. He smiled. 'Mrs Bartholomew, your boy has talent,' he said. 'Maybe we can use him. We'll let you know.'

She came back and told me. How I loathed that part of the business, the cap-in-hand uncertainty for the young artist, the condescension of management for his wares. I remember my mother rubbing the make-up off my face with spit. It was all so 'Don't call us, we'll call you,' that I was sure I had boobed. Not that I was at all sorry. Jack Hylton may have been God to a lot of people, but personally I couldn't have cared less. Though my mother will disagree and even present proof to back her contention, I still maintain I had no interest then in performing. It was a chore. Worse, at thirteen I felt a right Charlie, dressing up and putting on rouge, lipstick, eyebrow pencil and that nigger minstrel make-up which I knew was still round the back of my ears going home to Morecambe on the bus.

I'm grateful to my mother now. She pushed me into show business, and kept me there until she knew I was safely in Ernie's hands; he's been doing the pushing ever since.

My mother's motives were the highest. I was her only child, and if my father hadn't been so shy I could have been two years older.

'It's up to me to see that you are never tied to a whistle like your dad,' she used to say. Which was no disrespect to him. What she meant was that she had ambitions for me beyond the average run-of-the-mill working class fellow earning, like my father, around thirty-eight shillings a week as a labourer with the Morecambe Corporation.

Tall and easy-going, with a gentle disposition, my father was wholly content with his lot. How I envy him and his quiet dignity and philosophy, his simple pleasures, the respect and esteem of his work-mates and friends, and his supreme joy which he shared with my mother in watching the Turneresque sunset over

6

Morecambe Bay that they believe is the most magnificent in the world. He came of a stock which had bred into him a suspicion of the flash in the pan. Even after I could afford to keep him and my mother in comfort, and I constantly offered to do so, he held on to his job with the Corporation until he eventually retired—after over forty-five years' service.

My mother was the opposite. It's funny how memories of someone you've known all your life remain intact in vivid little scenes. My very first conscious memory of her was when I was literally a baby.

ERNIE His eyes didn't open till he was six months old.

ERIC The ceiling of our home in Morecambe had fallen in, and I remember being lifted on to the kitchen table by my mother and having my coat pulled on and my scarf tied round my neck, and being taken out of the house. That house was at 48, Buxton Street, Morecambe, where I was born. It was later condemned and we moved to alternative accommodation found for us by the Corporation at 43, Christie Avenue. The incredible part of it is that I could not have been more than nine or ten months old.

The next few years are hazy. This is where my mother has the last word, and my dad wouldn't dare contradict her!

I met Sadie and George Bartholomew, Eric's parents, at their house outside Morecambe. George was exactly as his son had described him. Sadie, who had inspired and helped create the Morecambe and Wise double-act, came as a fountain of amusing and intimate anecdote.

SADIE Politeness makes certain demands on me. I have to remember them. As for my son's saying I 'pushed' him into show business, my only reply is this, that he has even tried to sell *me* the same idea. I'm afraid that is not how I remember it. Eric loved show business and performing practically from the time he could walk, which he did at nine months. We had a gramophone and he knew every record we possessed. It's clear in my memory. He was like a little doll with a head of blond curls, and he soon learned to speak.

He would come in and say, 'What do you want playing?'

'Play me so and so,' I'd say.

He would go through the records, and though he couldn't read, he would find the very one I had named, put it on, and start dancing to it.

Whenever we took him out to relatives, all he wanted to do was perform. We entertained ourselves in those days—everyone had his or her party piece. Someone would sit at the piano. Immediately you'd see a blond curly top no higher than the keyboard.

'I want to do my party piece. I want to sing and dance.'

'Wait a minute, love,' he would be told.

I remember one particular night when the pianist told him to wait, and he said, 'All right, I'll wait under the table.' He must have been about three.

From time to time he would announce, 'I'm here, and I'm still waiting.'

Nobody paid much attention and he became as quiet as a mouse. When the time came to go, I said, 'Come along, Eric, run and get your coat.'

'But I haven't done my dance as yet,' he said.

'You can do it next time.'

'No, I want to do it tonight.'

'All right, then,' I said. 'Get on your feet and be quick about it.'

'But I am too tired to stand now,' he said. 'I will have to dance on my bottom.'

He was quite a handful. I didn't dare leave the front door open because he'd be off down the road. If I was taking him out, I found the best thing to do was to tie him by a scarf to the door-knob and let him sit on the step until I got ready. He had a little tam-o'-shanter with a pompom which I would put on his head, but he invariably pulled it off because he hated wearing it. One day he saw a sympathetic-looking man coming down the street, and he said, 'Look, I've tied myself too tight. Can you let me go?'

Unsuspecting, the man obliged. I came out to find the scarf hanging from the door-knob, but no Eric.

He was a flier—he could be anywhere. My first thought was to go straight to the police. I walked down to the bottom of Lancaster Road. Two old gentlemen were sitting on a bench.

'Have you seen a little boy go by?' I asked.

'Nay,' one of them replied, 'but we've seen a little lass with a curly top carrying a tammy.'

'That's him,' I said. 'Where is he?'

'Look,' said the other OAP, 'there he is, yonder.'

Eric was a little distance away, surrounded by a party of builders. They had rigged up a plank on a couple of crates and Eric was on it, going through his repertoire of nursery rhymes and even more sophisticated numbers like *Monterey* and *Dona Clara* and *Blue Moon* and *I'm Dancing With Tears in My Eyes* and heaven knows what else. The tammy was his box office and as far as I could see he was doing very well. His audience were loving it.

When I got there his little white suit was spattered with mud, his shoes and socks were caked where he had squelched through a really sticky patch, and his face was filthy.

He saw me and announced to his audience, 'I'd better go now, there's me Mam.'

One of the builders said, 'That little lad's a wonderful entertainer.'

'I'll *entertain* him when I get him home,' I said.

'Oh,' said Eric, 'that means I will have to have my bottom slapped, won't I, Mum?'

'You've never spoken a truer word.'

'Well, folks,' said Eric to his audience, 'I'll have to be going. Goodbye everybody. See you tomorrow.'

'Over my dead body,' said I. To Eric, 'You are filthy.'

'It's been worth it,' he said. 'Look at all those pennies. Has my dad come home?'

'Wait till I get you in. You will taste the strap.'

On the way back we stopped at a shop owned by an old friend, Mrs Pascoe. I went in for a chat with her. Eric went behind the counter and emerged with a dog lead. 'Better give me the strap now,' he said. 'It won't hurt so much with Mrs Pascoe looking.'

I think I can say Eric's childhood was happy. Naturally he was deprived, like every only child, of the companionship of brothers and sisters, but he was never short of friends of his own age because there were plenty of neighbours' children around us, and he had a wonderful relationship with his father. The snag was

9

that, although Eric was a born entertainer with always a ready reply and more than his fair share of cheek, he was no student. His school reports were our despair.

ERIC I wasn't just hopeless in class, I was terrible. I went to two Morecambe schools, the Lancaster Road Junior School and, after that, the Euston Road Senior School. My mother was very keen for me to go to a grammar school—she believed in education. But the headmaster told her, 'Mrs Bartholomew, I've been teaching boys for thirty years. Take my advice. It would be a complete waste of time.'

'I'm willing to pay for his further education,' my mother said.

'It would be money down the drain,' the headmaster replied.

I readily agreed with him. I hadn't put my hand up in class except when I was hopping from one foot to the other. But to be honest I wasn't worried. I had no bright ambitions. To me my future was clear. At fifteen I would get myself a paper round.

At seventeen I would learn to read it. And at eighteen I would get a job on the Corporation like my dad. I'd go to the cinema on Saturday nights and out in a boat fishing on Sundays. What more could a man ask?

My mother had other plans, and they were laid when I was ten. On that day my cousin Peggy, three years older than me, had called at the house—her parents lived just up the road, at 21, Christie Avenue.

'Auntie Sadie, I'm going to dancing class on Saturday,' she told my mother.

'Rather you than me,' I remarked.

My mother said, 'Where's that?'

'Miss Hunter's, above the Plaza. A shilling a lesson.'

'Do me a favour,' said my mother, 'take Eric with you.'

'I could kill you,' I told Peggy. 'Matter of fact, I have worked out the perfect crime and you'll be my first victim.'

The trouble with me is that although I make plans—wonderful plans based on brilliant ideas—I never seem to be able to get around to carrying them out. Cousin Peggy survived. Not only that, she called for me the following Saturday, all goody-goody, and I was taken to Miss Hunter's dancing school.

I was the only boy in the class which meant I was a target for gibes in and out of school. There were times when it was really awful, in addition to which I begrudged the dancing school every moment it took me away from play, but my mother made me stick it out. I learnt a bit of tap dancing and was soon able to go with the class to church functions called 'pies and peas', a well-known institution in the North, whereby children entertain OAPs and are given in return a meal of hot meat pies and peas.

Miss Hunter's report on my progress must have been encouraging because I next found myself going for singing lessons (I have the world's worst voice), and music lessons. I was put to learning the piano, the piano accordion, the guitar, the clarinet, the trumpet, even the euphonium, none of which I ever managed to play even badly, though my mother worked hard to pay for it all.

She was a waitress at the Café Royal in Morecambe, then an usherette at the Central Pier Theatre. The names on the bills? How well I remember them. Comedians like Harry Neil, Hedley Claxton, Teddy Williams, Jimmy Charteris, with all sorts of other acts and a line of chorus girls one of whom was somehow always called Mona.

I marvel now at the effort and sacrifice that went into preparing me for show business, for in addition to her job my mother also worked as a daily help, dusting and cleaning at three or four houses every week in order to pay for my lessons.

One night she came back after seeing Miss Hunter who lived fairly close by, in Roseberry Avenue. Their conversation had gone something like this:

'It's about my Eric. I've come to ask you how he's getting along at the dancing.'

'Very well, Mrs Bartholomew. Yes, very well, considering . . .'

'What do you mean?'

'Well, he might make quite a good dancer—*eventually*. You see, he can't learn very much in one hour every Saturday with all the girls there.'

So my mother said, 'How much are your private lessons?'

'Half a crown an hour.'

'All right then, put him down for one private lesson every week as well.'

Miss Hunter did, and not long after that my complaining about the dancing school suddenly ceased.

There was a girl in the class called Molly Bunting, about a year and a half older than me, with pink round cheeks, big blue eyes, a pouting rosebud for a mouth and a pert nose that always seemed to sniff the air above her whenever I went near.

After a few private hours at the dancing school, Miss Hunter said she thought it might be a good idea if Molly Bunting came as well as she wanted to train us in a dance act. I was thrilled. The act was a straight lift of the Fred Astaire and Ginger Rogers routines. Their musical films were the rage in those days. Soon Molly and I were dancing to those wonderful tunes, *Cheek to Cheek, I Won't Dance, Let's Face the Music and Dance, Smoke Gets in Your Eyes. . . .*

Now dancing classes were glimpses of heaven. I was head over heels in love with Molly. My mother must have known it, because, whenever we went to perform at a 'pies and peas', she came too, to see there was no hanky panky. I wasn't but eleven. I wonder if she had seen signs of some remarkable precocity. She has never said. It was about this time that my mother and father took me to a social at the Jubilee Club, which was a working men's club in Torrisholme, just outside Morecambe.

The concert secretary came to my father. 'I hear your Eric does a bit of a turn?'

'Aye,' said my father, 'he sings and things.'

'Do you think he could do something here next Saturday dinner time?'

'I think so.'

'How much will you want?'

'Oh, he'll do it for nothing,' said my father, who has always believed the word revolves on brotherly love.

'Oh no,' said the concert secretary, 'we are quite willing to pay him.'

They settled on five shillings which was the first money I ever earned for doing my thing. I seemed to go down well because I was booked again for the following week.

That started me working the clubs. We got a special licence for me to perform from the Education Committee on the strength of my father's being practically teetotal. For a Saturday dinner time and Saturday evening we used to get, I think, fifteen shillings to a pound, which was quite an addition to the family budget.

Next we started building up my solo act—G. H. Elliott's *Lily of Laguna*, in a white suit with my face smeared with burnt cork, and the ghastly *I'm Not All There*—but I was never happy doing it. Naturally, I liked getting laughs, but honestly I don't think I ever actually started enjoying my work as a performer until after I became a name and it started being a good thing financially. Until then it was just a job that only on some nights felt even middling good.

I was able to add my impression of Flanagan and Allen to my act after seeing them at the Winter Garden Theatre in Morecambe. I waited at the stage door and got their autographs, which I still have. Years later, Ernie and I were with them in a Royal Command Performance, and I was able to tell them how I had pirated their act.

'You can pay us back,' Bud said, 'by giving us *your* autograph.' I was thrilled. It was a wonderful compliment.

Besides working the clubs as far afield as Preston and Lancaster, and steadily doing better and better financially, I then joined an outfit called Billy Baxter and his Band. Billy bought me a silver-grey dress suit, and I used to sing with the band, believe it or not, at the Grosvenor Hotel and the Broadway Hotel in Morecambe. The actress, Diana Coupland, a Morecambe girl, remembers me at the Grosvenor. She mentioned it when we met not long ago. I had thought I'd be able to live that one down, but it is a small world.

My mother had started entering me in talent contests. There was a concert party on the sea front at Morecambe called the Nigger Minstrels. They ran a contest which I won three years running. I don't claim I was all that good, but I was the only child performer among grown men and women—whistlers, mouth organ players, Irish club singers, impressionists who did things like trains in tunnels, sword dancers and the like. Besides, they were nearly all visitors while I was a local boy with a powerful lobby of relatives and friends. Eventually I was banned from taking part as visiting competitors were being discouraged.

I was then able to rest on my Laurels and Hardys and watch the others rather patronisingly from the front row.

There were other local competitions, however, in cinemas and ballrooms. Many of these I also won in those whirlwind years. Then came the Hoylake contest, and its anti-climax of a 'prize'— being auditioned by Jack Hylton three months later.

My mother had been told by Hylton that they would let us know, but as the weeks passed her hopes began to fade—until a good three months later came another telegram, addressed to my mother, asking if her son Eric Bartholomew could appear at the Nottingham Empire as one of Bryan Michie's Discoveries in the touring show, *Youth Takes a Bow*. Salary—£5 a week plus travelling expenses for the two of us as she was expected to accompany me.

I must have been in this show about two months when a rumour went around that Ernie Wise was joining it at Swansea. To us Ernie Wise was a big star. He had appeared in the West End and he had been on the BBC with a radio version of *Youth Takes a Bow*. I remember sitting at home, even before I won the contest at Hoylake, listening to Ernie Wise and a girl called Mary Naylor on the radio with Arthur Askey and Stinker Murdoch on Monday nights at seven.

Mary was now in the touring version of *Youth Takes a Bow*, and her account of Ernie's brilliance as an entertainer—a pretty girl like Mary carrying such a torch for the guy—immediately gave me an acutely jealous inferiority complex.

He boarded the train at Crewe, if I remember rightly. I saw him all smiles and bounce going along the corridor, saying hello to the discoveries he knew, and finally settling in and taking possession of Mary, the choicest discovery of them all.

I didn't meet him until the following morning, a Monday, at band call at the Swansea Empire. Somebody's mother introduced him to my mother and I was there. I think he said 'Hi' very breezily and bounced off. There was a café with a pin-table next door to the theatre. We all congregated in there, and I think he paid a penny for me to have a go on the pin-table, which on looking back seems almost incredible.

He was taller than me at the time, and in long trousers—he had just turned fifteen, and this of course meant he was no longer having to attend school: unlike myself, a mere schoolboy still in shorts, whose school attendances had to be certified in every town we visited. On top of that his mother wasn't with him so he was not attached to any apron strings. All of which gave him a debonair and, to my mind, devastating advantage with the girls. I remember standing in the wings of the Swansea Empire, watching Ernie in his immaculate, made-to-measure dress suit and straw hat, singing songs like *Elmer's Tune* and *Run Rabbit Run*. He was good too, no doubt about that, and he could do a good tap dance. He looked so assured, a real Mickey Rooney, and I remember thinking, Bighead.

I little realised that under his bumptious and cocky exterior the real Ernie Wise was homesick and missed his father with whom he had done a double-act practically from the time he could stand. My mother had spotted it, though. Few people can fool my mother.

2

Eᴙɴɪᴇ So it's my turn at last to get a word in edgewise. First of all, yes to that last remark from Eric. His mother was so right. Although I was taller and better looking than her envious son— they were injecting him with giraffe hormone to make him grow —I was basically shy, sensitive and self-effacing. I still am. Home was far away at 12, Station Terrace, East Ardsley, between Wakefield and Leeds, where my family lived. Dad was a railway porter and signal lampman, the product of very poor circumstances. His father died when he was fourteen and his mother was blind. In World War I, he had joined the Army, at sixteen, by adding two years to his age, and won the Military Medal for saving his sergeant's life. I used to ply him with questions about it—I have always been fascinated by war and love reading war books—but I could never get him to talk about his experiences. He was a wonderful personality but absolutely hopeless with money, a big bone of contention with my mother who was always a very thrifty person. She needed to be, on my father's wage of less than £2 a week with five children to feed and clothe.

Her family were better off. Her father earned £10 a week, big money sixty years ago, making warps for the weavers in a woollen mill. One of the weavers was my mother who started work three days after she left school at thirteen, rapidly rising to become a skilled box-loom weaver, producing lovely soft serge and worsteds, at a wage of £3 a week.

ERIC Note how he keeps harping on wages. Money is his obsession. It was his big motivation in our pursuit of that elusive and mythical creature, the Wooslem Bird of success.

ERNIE I'll choose to ignore that. I'll return to my maternal grandfather.

ERIC I've heard of him. I'm not saying he was mean but he wouldn't even spend Christmas.

ERNIE (*patiently*) A dour man. Yes that and hard, of the sort only Yorkshire breeds.

ERIC Aye.

ERNIE He never had any time for my father, a spendthrift and worse, a spendthrift who had tripped over his eldest daughter Connie's umbrella on a tram and immediately taken her fancy. She was then nearly twenty-four and it was mainly my grandfather's opposition to my father that pushed her into marrying him.

She had worked hard for nigh on ten years, during which time the only pocket money she had ever received from my grandfather, out of her own wage packet, was five shillings a week. Aye, and out of that too she was expected to save, and she did.

'I'll cut you off if you marry him. I'll make sure no worthless husband of yours gets a penny of my money,' he had warned her. 'You're my favourite daughter, but you'll get nowt from me.'

And she got nowt. He changed his will in favour of my mother's two sisters, my Auntie Nellie and my Auntie Annie, who inherited all he possessed when he died.

All my mother took with her from her home were her clothes and her piano which she had bought out of her savings—she played beautifully. She has it still in her flat in Leeds with framed photographs of her children, and Eric, and my father on it.

She and my father first lived in lodgings—a single room for which they paid six shillings a week. They then managed to rent a house in Warder Street in Leeds, a one up and one down for eight shillings a week, but in order to secure the lease they had to pay £12 for the installation of a fixture, a gas geyser.

My early memories are of this house; indeed the first thing I actually remember was an accident that happened just outside

17

the house when a motorcycle crashed and a girl who was riding pillion bruised her knee pretty badly. My dad, who was a member of the St John's Ambulance Brigade, rushed for his first-aid kit and bandaged her up.

From Warder Street we moved to Kingsley, near Hemsworth. Then, when I was about five, to East Ardsley. Our house in East Ardsley was below the railway line which was up on an embankment overlooking our patch at the back with its outside loo, the outhouse with my mother's copper boiler, and the wooden shed in which I kept my rabbits. Whenever a train went past, the place shook. We didn't mind that, though. We were a railway family. In fact, I used to love the feeling of a train thundering past. It was nice and exciting.

My father's mother stayed with us at one time in a back room, a plump little woman who had lost her sight, we were told, because of some neglect on the part of the midwife when she was pregnant. I remember she loved a peach; my father used to bring her one from time to time, and if I was around she always gave me a piece of it.

I remember as a child playing on her bed, rolling and jumping about, and she would say, 'I hope you don't pee in your bath water.'

'Oh no, Nana.'

'Because that would give you creepy crawlies.'

I have always remembered that and I have never peed in the bath water. I don't know about the others, though, on Saturday nights when the galvanised iron bath would be brought into the kitchen, hot water poured in from the big black kettle, and the whole family, boys and girls, and finally mother and father took a bath.

I was the oldest child. Then came Gordon, now a farmer outside Cambridge, then Ann, a teacher in Leeds, then Constance, who has emigrated with her family to Australia, and finally Arthur, who died as a child.

The kitchen was the living room with a coal range which kept the room warm and the oven hot; a happy, homely, reassuring place, where my mother cooked and we had our meals and we washed our hands and faces and she washed up in the kitchen sink. Every detail of that room is still clear in my mind's eye after more than thirty years.

In addition, there was the front room with my mother's piano, and there were two rooms upstairs. Below the pavement was a coal cellar which you entered from a flight of steps at one side. In other words, a typical poorer working-class house in a Coronation Street. It was lit by gas. I'm trying to set the scene. I want you to get to know us and how we lived before I tell you what we did.

Breakfast was usually bread and dripping, and that went for tea when, occasionally, there might also be a boiled egg. The big meal was dinner, at midday, for which my mother usually made a stew in a saucepan as large as a wash-basin with perhaps fifteen or sixteen large dumplings. We ate a lot of rice pudding—she would put a pint of milk into a pudding and bake it in the oven with a grating of nutmeg and a flavouring of vanilla. Does that make your mouth water? It does mine.

Sunday dinner was the meal of the week. It began with a huge, hot Yorkshire pudding which you ate with steaming gravy. Then came the meat, veg and potatoes, and finally probably a caramel custard.

Monday was washday. Mother rose at six and went to the outhouse where she lit a fire under her copper boiler and in it she boiled the clothes in soapy water. The wash would be done by eight o'clock. It was pegged out to dry, then ironed with a heavy flat iron that had to be heated from time to time on the range. That day you got what she called a shuffle dinner.

'You'll all have to shuffle today,' she'd say. Shuffle dinner would be cold meat and potatoes.

By the time we reached East Ardsley, my mother's father had retired from the mill and bought an ale house at Farsley with a stone floor and wooden benches. It was called the New Inn, though he continued to live in Pudsey in a stone cottage. His sport was bowls, and I believe he once played the trombone. We used to visit him and my grandmother. I, for my part, ever hoping for a miracle, a tip from my grandfather, but it never happened. By then even my grandmother, despairing of ever receiving enough for the housekeeping, was helping herself from the till.

Then she died, and I was taken to Pudsey to see her, laid out in the bedroom from which all the furniture had been removed. She was in her coffin supported on two chairs with her hands joined as if in prayer. She looked marvellous, I thought, with her pink cheeks and white forehead, rather like the waxworks of Eric and myself in Madame Tussaud's, but with her face framed by her gentle white hair. As a child, all curiosity, I was fascinated. But years later when my father died I couldn't bear the thought of seeing him laid out like that and only went into the room after the lid had been screwed down on his coffin.

He had meant too much to me alive for me to be able to look on his waxen face in death. Our relationship had really developed as a double-act. He was something of an entertainer, and I remember as a small child watching him perform at working men's clubs to make a little extra money. I wanted to follow his example. One day I said to my mother, 'Come on, Ma, teach me a song.'

She is a lively little person, with a big smile, always brimming over with enthusiasm, and pure Yorkshire. She put down what she was doing and we went into the front room. She sat at her piano and ruffled through a pile of sheet music—you could buy a song in those days for sixpence.

'Well, what's it to be?'

'What about *The Sheikh of Araby*?' I said.

We went over the song a few times until I learnt the words.

'Now you go on rehearsing it,' she said. 'When your dad comes home, you can do it for him.'

That evening after tea my mother said to my father, 'Go into the front room. Ernest has something to show you.'

He went out and my mother took a towel and tied it over my head with a piece of string.

'Wait for me to play the introduction, then come in for the song,' she said. 'Put your heart and soul into it.'

'OK, Ma.'

I heard the opening chords, dashed in too soon and fell over a chair.

'Go out and let's try it again,' said my mother.

Which I did. It went fine, and I will never forget the reaction I got from my father. He was bowled over, so excited and thrilled that his eldest son had taken after him and had a spark of talent that there were tears in his eyes.

After that he started to train me for stage work. It was the age of child Hollywood stars, and the one hope, I suppose, was that I would emulate them. I remember we both went for tap-dancing lessons. Before long I was going around the clubs with my father doing cross-talk and songs. It's hard to be exact about dates. Thinking back, I could not have been much older than six.

What remains most vividly in my memory is a sort of composite picture of those working men's clubs—Labour, Conservative, union-run or specific to a factory or trade: a big main room with usually a long bar running along one side and a stage, the room filled with marble-topped, cast-iron tables, chairs and against the wall, benches. There'd be a snooker room and a place where you played darts. There'd be fruit machines. There'd be beer and sandwiches, pies, potato crisps, pickles and bottles of tomato sauce, the whole place crowded for the concert with working-class people dressed in their Sunday best. The men wore blue serge suits, white shirts with detachable, boned collars and patterned ties fastened to the shirt front by a clip, pocket handkerchiefs to match, black shoes and short hair slicked down. The women and girls wore home-made dresses, their hair in tight curls still smelling faintly of heated tongs, and the bolder, unmarried ones wore make-up. There'd be a scattering of children running about, getting in the way of waiters in white coats and long white aprons carrying trays laden with drinks, mainly beer; if they were paid with a note, you'd see them holding it in their teeth till they had produced the correct change. In the middle of it all there'd be the concert secretary at a table near the stage ringing his official bell and saying, 'Now give order for the next act on the bill which is going to be, ladies and gentlemen— CARSON AND KID!'

Which was the stage name my father and I adopted. Later we became Bert Carson and his Little Wonder.

We'd go on and sing numbers together like *It Happened on the Beach at Bali Bali* and *Walking in a Winter Wonderland*. I had one or two songs I sang on my own like *I'm Knee Deep in Daisies* and *Let's Have a Tiddly at the Milk Bar*.

Then we'd do our cross-talk, material taken from Christmas crackers and early joke books:

Carson   Excuse me, but I went for a walk.

Kid   You went for a fork?

Carson   I got as far as my uncle's—

Kid   Where you pawned the fork.

      (*My uncle's was a local term for a pawnbroker*)

Carson   Hi, Kid.

Kid   Hi, Carson.

Carson   What's that you were saying about the two miners (*or mill workers or farmers, depending on where you worked*) you saw t'other day?

Kid   They were sitting on the street corner.

Carson   On street corner?

Kid   Aye. And one said, 'What shall we do today?'

Carson   What did t'other say?

Kid   He said, 'I don't know.'

Carson   So what did the first miner say?

Kid   He said, 'I'll tell you what. Let's toss a coin. If it comes down heads, we'll go to the football match. If it comes down tails, we'll go dog-racing. And if it stands on edge, we'll go to work.'

That was the level of our comedy. Eric would probably call it Primitive Wise.

ERIC   I'll go so far as to call it the Best of Wise.

ERNIE   For our second spot my father would put on a white suit and blacken his face—there was usually a dressing room near the stage. We would then sing songs like *Little Pal*, a great tear-jerker, with me sitting on his knee.

The Holbeck Working Men's Club, near the Leeds United ground, was the local show date, rather like what the Metropolitan Theatre, Edgware Road, was to variety in London. All the variety agents in London went to the Met; all the club concert secretaries in Leeds and for a radius of thirty miles around went to Holbeck. The moment you finished your act at Holbeck, they would stand up and wave, and my father would go to their tables with our date book. There might be a bit of haggling over five shillings but our average was a pound for a Saturday night and thirty shillings for Sunday dinner-time and Sunday night, making two pounds ten shillings for the two days. That was more than my father earned for the rest of the week.

For one of my numbers I wore red wooden clogs, a familiar article of footwear in Yorkshire for generations. Believe it or not, in the old days men fought clog duels in which two opponents gripped each other by the shoulders and started kicking each other's shins till one of them called it a day.

With the clogs I wore a comedy check suit. In another act which I developed later I wore a Charlie Chaplin outfit, with a bowler hat and a black 'tash.

The snag as far as I was concerned was that my father took all the money for a performance. So I got the idea of giving friends of mine in the audience pennies to throw on the stage when I was out alone. This would start others in the audience doing the same and by the end of the act I might collect two shillings in coppers which I stashed away in a corner of my cupboard. One or two pennies I'd spend on chocolates at four for a penny or spice (sweets) at eight for a penny. The rest of the money I saved. In a few years I had over a hundred pounds, and I have never lost the habit of saving.

My father and I paid for our family holidays at Cleethorpes, on the Lincolnshire coast, by performing at two big clubs there for which we were paid £7 a night. There was a wonderful family spirit about Northern clubs in those days when beer at 1s. 2d. (6p) a pint was the only drink members could afford, and there was always good-hearted encouragement for the performer who tried his best. People were generous, too. Usually if we were booked for a Sunday dinner-time show somebody would say, 'You must come home and have dinner with us.'

In a mining town the food would be good, and there would be plenty of it. The fire in the front room would be good too, with the coal heaped high up the chimney—miners received a large ration of free coal.

I remember vividly, at one miner's home, meeting his only child, a boy of nineteen, who had spent most of his life in a bed in a back room. He had a ghastly white skin as though sunlight had never touched it, and he shook all the time. The parents brought him downstairs to have his dinner with us, but his movements were so badly articulated that he could not get the food to his mouth and in the end his mother had to feed him. I was too upset to eat my dinner, which is saying something.

For high tea in a miner's household it was usually John West tinned salmon followed by pineapple chunks and custard with, of course, plenty of bread and butter on the table, a chocolate or walnut cake, and more often than not an oven-bottomed cake. An oven-bottomed cake is a type of bread I have seen only in Yorkshire. It is round and large, larger in fact than an LP record, and flat but risen in the middle. The housewives leave them to cool on the front doorstep where the odd dog might add a bit of flavour. Never mind, with plenty of butter on a slice of it you'll forget the dog. Another treat was parkin, a wonderful spiced ginger cake. There was always parkin on bonfire night.

Now, I've eaten the great Lancashire dishes that they are so proud of—hotpot, Hindel wakes (chicken stuffed with apples and simmered for two days in cider), and tripe and onions (eaten hot in Lancashire but preferred cold in Yorkshire with vinegar, salt and pepper). All excellent, but when you boil it down it's each man to his own so let's not argue. Meanwhile, give me a Yorkshire pork pie made by an honest-faced butcher in a moorland village and you can say what you like about Melton Mowbray pies.

Getting back to working men's clubs on Sunday evenings there would be our second show with always the hope we would be able to leave in time to catch the last bus home. If we missed that, Monday mornings were sheer agony. I remember being lifted out of bed and dressed while I was still virtually asleep, given food I couldn't eat in that state, and set on my way to school where I promptly fell asleep. Result—a letter from the Leeds education authorities informing my parents that exploiting juveniles was against the law and was to stop forthwith. A serious blow to the family at that period. In fact we couldn't do without the money. So we got around the difficulty by transferring our activities from Leeds to Bradford.

This increased our transport problem. Many were the nights

on which we missed the last bus and I wound up being carried several miles on my father's back and our getting home at one or two in the morning.

School was at Thorpe, two miles away. I walked it, in lace-up boots and stockings that always seemed to disappear into my boots by the time I got there, and I walked home for dinner during the midday break. I loved that school. The headmaster was a Mr Riley. He had been gassed during World War I which was why, we were told, his eyes continually wept. He was kind and occasionally rewarded boys who got a difficult question right.

One day he asked the class, 'Why do not the seas around Britain freeze in winter?' He looked at me. 'You Ernest Wiseman. You answer that.'

I stood up, happy, confident. It was one of the big incidents in a scholastic career that was, I promise you, in no way distinguished.

'Because of the Gulf Stream Drift from the Gulf of Mexico, sir,' I said.

'Correct,' said Mr Riley, and he presented me with a half-penny in front of the whole class. A half-penny bought four spice. My weekly pocket money was only a penny.

ERIC And he saved out of that.

ERNIE Those were the days when school milk was first introduced—a half-pint a day with a ginger biscuit per child for which parents were expected to contribute twopence-halfpenny (1p) a week. How times have changed.

From that happy junior school, I was moved to Ardsley Boys' School, a rougher place, run by a vinegar-faced headmaster who could see what was going on behind him by using the corner of his glasses as you do wing mirrors on a car, and he would pay you back in his own good time for misdemeanours you hoped had escaped his notice. He would creep up behind you when you least expected it and tweak your ear.

From his form I moved up into that of a man we called the Toad. The Toad hated me.

'Come out, tap dancer,' he would order me. I have never heard the words 'tap dancer' uttered with more contempt. I used to feel it badly.

Even then, entertaining was a sort of personality prop which helped me to cover up a deep-rooted shyness and sense of inadequacy. Entertaining brought me out of myself. The moment I put on my comedy suit, I was able to step out of my very private little world and be an entirely different person, a cheeky chappie.

I remember at a club, sitting with my father with people in the audience who had invited us to their table. I was asked what I would have to drink and I said I would like a grapefruit juice, and my father accepted his usual, a half-pint of Tetley's beer.

A big song hit at the time was *The Greatest Mistake of my Life*. Everybody was singing or humming it. Someone at the table said to me, 'Boy, your flies are open.'

I looked down. 'Yes,' I said, 'it's *the greatest mistake of my life!*'

I'll never forget the laugh I got, but if I hadn't been in a comedy suit I could never have made a crack like that.

Two things move me very deeply. For some reason, one is an act of kindness. At one of the club raffles the first prize was a budgerigar. I must have looked at it very longingly because the concert secretary said, 'All right, son, the next time you perform at this club you shall have a budgie like it.'

It was nearly a year before we went back to that club, but the man had not forgotten his promise. After the show there was a budgie in a cage for me to take away. I was thrilled beyond words. I took it home. In the bedroom I let it out of the cage—I have never liked to see any creature confined. Next morning I went off to school, leaving the budgie in the bedroom outside its cage. I hadn't warned my mother about it, and the inevitable happened. She came upstairs to do out the room, opened the window as she always did, and the budgie promptly took off.

That evening my father and I spent hours wandering about the roads calling, 'Budgie, Budgie', but not a hope. We eventually gave up the search and I wept, not so much for the loss of my budgie but because, I remember it clearly, the kindness of the concert secretary in giving it to me.

I suppose it was the consciousness of being poor that produced this reaction to kindness in me. Poverty is of itself fate's classic act of unkindness to a human creature. It gets ingrained in you. You are so conditioned by poverty to expect the worst that any unexpected gesture that argues you are wrong about the world and the people in it is very moving. At least I find it so.

By the same token, the reverse, unfairness, has always provoked in me a very deep sense of anger. One day the Toad caned a boy whose classwork was chronically bad. The boy was crying. We saw great bloodshot weals on the back of his thighs. On investigating further, we found his buttocks literally black and blue. I was so shocked—the boy was not very bright—that I took him around Ardsley, showing the marks to parents with children at the school. Thinking back, I can hardly believe I possessed such nerve—I have never been one to jump in at the deep end. I could not have been more than eleven.

The Toad got to hear of my campaign because a complaint was made, but he never said a word about it to me. In fact it made him a little wary of me after that because I ceased hearing myself referred to contemptuously as the tap dancer.

Like Eric I took part in talent contests, and I too had my share of 'pies and peas'. Maybe it's the enchantment of early memories, but I have never tasted hot meat pies like those I was given as a child for helping to entertain old folks.

But the event that attracted the most interest in our neck of the woods, with the Lord Mayor there and reports in the press, was an annual charity show at the Bradford Alhambra called *The Nignog Revue*.

The Nignogs were a reader's club for children run by a Bradford paper, *The Telegraph and Argus*, with an Uncle and Auntie who wrote a column, answered our letters and sent us a badge to wear.

I recall being the only Nignog who was paid to take part in the revue—because my parents were badly off. That was in September 1936 when we packed the Alhambra which could seat 2,000—the profits went to the King George Memorial Playing Fields Fund. It was my first appearance on a theatre stage, but what I remember most vividly of the occasion was the party after the show with lots of wonderful things to eat, and a brown paper parcel of goodies in which we found little presents. In mine, a penknife, pencil and a pullover. I was in the show again in 1937 and 1938.

Next we read that a man named Bryan Michie was holding

auditions at the Leeds Empire in a search for amateur talent. I went to the theatre all on my own. I gave my name to the stage door keeper. He regarded me suspiciously but anyhow passed me on through a chain of command until I found myself on the stage in front of a big plump man with curly hair sitting in the front stalls. The next thing I knew I was in London with my father—under contract to Jack Hylton.

Even now, thirty-five years later, that thrilling succession of events has a fairy-tale quality. A room was booked for us at the Shaftesbury Hotel near Trafalgar Square. It was my first hotel, magically and wonderfully luxurious with around every corner and corridor something new and exciting to be explored. Even going to the lavatory was an adventure because a light came on in your cubicle every time you shut the door.

Unhappily for me my father insisted on going back to Leeds after a week. Jack Hylton was keen for him to stay on in London. There was a job going for him at a much better wage than he got from the railway, but Dad did not feel it was right to leave the rest of the family.

I opened at the Princes Theatre in London on Friday 7 January, 1939, in Jack Hylton's show *Band Waggon* with Arthur Askey at the top of the bill, and I woke next morning to find my name in all the national newspapers. I had to pinch myself to make sure I wasn't dreaming. FAME IN A NIGHT FOR 13-YEAR-OLD was one headline. Another, COMEDIAN, 13, HAILED AS A GREAT DISCOVERY. And another, RAILWAY PORTER'S SON STAR OVERNIGHT.

There were write-ups like 'Ernie Wise—one quarter Max Miller, one quarter Sydney Howard, and the other half a mixture of all the comics who ever amused you—wears a squashed-in billycock hat, striped black and grey city trousers (too small for him), a black frock coat with a pink carnation in the buttonhole, grey spats and brown clogs. His timing and confidence are remarkable. At thirteen he is an old-time performer.'

And 'He came on without a sign of nerves, full of Yorkshire cockiness; sang—in a voice that made microphones unnecessary —*I'm Knee Deep in Daisies* and *Let's Have a Tiddly at the Milk Bar*; cracked a pair of North Country jokes; and did a whirlwind step dance with terrific aplomb and efficiency. He is a sort of Yorkshire Max Miller, tilts his battered bowler over one arm and has a wicked wink. Off-stage he gives an even better performance. He lives between Leeds and Wakefield. 'Isn't Wakefield the prison where they play cricket?' Someone asked him.

' "Aye," he came back without hesitation, "but the warders always win!" '

It was Jack Hylton who invented my stage name Wise. My contract with him was for five years, starting on £6 a week, twice as much as my father earned then as a parcels clerk at Leeds Central Station. After he returned to Leeds, I felt very alone and insecure; we had always been together and were very close. However, Jack Hylton took his place in a way. He saw to it that I was well looked after. I stayed in a flat above the Fifty-Fifty Restaurant, in St Martin's Lane, in the charge of a Mrs Rodway, who was also responsible for two other juveniles in the show— Maureen Potter, who is now a big star in Ireland, and Maureen Flanagan. They also lived above the restaurant. Mrs Rodway drew my wages, out of which she sent three pounds home, paid twenty-five shillings for my digs and meals, which she cooked, gave me five shillings a week spending money, and banked the rest. I kept the bank book.

When the show went on tour in May 1939, Mrs Rodway came too, as our foster mother. She fixed our digs and the four of us always stayed together. We had to be out of the theatre by ten every night, and in bed soon after. In every town we visited the education authorities had to be notified. We had to attend school, but you can imagine what we were able to learn going to a different school every week. What usually happened was that we wound up reading a book at the back of the class.

As often as not we would come out of school for the midday break and step into Jack Hylton's chauffeur-driven Buick waiting for us in the road outside. We would be whisked off to the theatre for a brief rehearsal. We would then have lunch (it was no longer called dinner), after which we would be taken back to school.

Jack Hylton was wonderful to me. Some days I would get a message to go to his dressing room—he was actually performing in the show with his band. I would find him sitting before a pile of cold tripe and I would be invited to help him finish it. Or he would give me a generous hunk of pork pie—one arrived for him every week from a butcher he knew in Bolton, Lancashire. He was a typical Lancashireman, very down-to-earth, always picking his nose and scratching his arse.

ERIC Don't get the idea that all Lancashiremen pick their noses and scratch their arses. Some of us do it the other way about.

ERNIE We all have our endearing little quirks, but let's not digress. I am talking about a very successful man who was very kind to me.

Perhaps he saw in me a reflection of his own childhood because he too started from a very poor background—in Bolton, playing the piano in pubs. I remember he once saw me shivering in a thin raincoat; next day I had a thick overcoat. Then, in Newcastle, I found myself being taken into a big department store by his manager who had instructions to fit me out with a complete wardrobe, from head to toe, with sets of underwear, socks, shirts, ties, the lot, even two new suitcases in which to pack all this gear.

Seeing me properly dressed after that may have had something to do with it, but a week or two later Jack Hylton decided that I should come out of my clogs and comedy outfit. In Sheffield, an order was placed with a tailor named Barney Goodman to make me my first dinner suit—a dapper white jacket with black trousers which I wore with a Maurice Chevalier straw hat.

I remained in the show until it came to an end when the war broke out and the theatres were closed. But instead of sending me home to my parents in East Ardsley Jack Hylton took me to Kingston Gorse, his big house at Angmering-on-Sea, where I lived as one of the family which included Fifi, his Austrian wife, and Jackie and Georgia, his two daughters. There were three servants.

Neighbours, whom we saw a lot of, were the big West End impresario, George Black, with his children, George, Alfred and Paula.

Never a week went by without Jack's giving me five shillings pocket money. I stayed quite a while. Then I began to get homesick. In my absence, my youngest brother Arthur had died of peritonitis. He was only five. Besides, my father was no longer a fit man. Working the clubs with me had been his life, and he hadn't been the same since I left. He had tried to get my brother Gordon and my sisters to perform. Annie could play the piano quite well, but apparently it was impossible to get any of them on to a stage. Later my father developed rheumatoid arthritis from which he never really recovered.

Eventually I went to Jack Hylton and asked if I could go home to my family.

'Of course,' he said.

He paid for my ticket back to Leeds, but I'll not forget how upset I was when my father greeted me with, 'Why did you come home? You had it made.'

Eventually the theatres re-opened and show business started up again. Jack Hylton brought me back to London, this time to appear on the radio shows Eric has mentioned. After that I joined the touring version of *Youth Takes a Bow*, and at Swansea met Eric and his mother. Soon fate and Sadie Bartholomew were to take a hand in shaping our lives together.

3

ERIC You can 'sell' a discoveries show in various ways. The appeal lies in its degree of audience identification. If a discovery is bad the audience say, 'How terrible,' but feel good; if the discovery is good they feel they can do as well if not better given half the chance. The late Carrol Levis made a point of holding auditions in every town he toured—it was part of his advance publicity. But the basis of the show was always a hard core of 'discovery' talent that he or theatrical agents who toured with it had spotted.

Bryan Michie worked differently. He made up his discoveries bill from talent, mainly children, whom he had auditioned in advance. They appeared in the second half; the first half was made up of professional variety acts who were paid the market rate for the job. The rest of us, the young discoveries especially, were well and truly exploited.

I was on £5 plus free travel for myself and my mother which in any case was obtained at a discount from the railway on a block booking. Even Ernie was on only £7 a week. There was a yawning gap between that and Bryan Michie's salary of three figures a week, with first class travel, and of course Jack Hylton's three-figure profits even with front stalls at only four shillings and sixpence as they were in those days. For we were doing great business—children, in that age of the Shirley Temple hangover, were a big draw. And Ernie had a bigger hangover and bigger drawers than Shirley Temple ever had.

The star of the discoveries was Mary Naylor, just six months older than Ernie but a lot prettier. She used to come on with her piano accordion singing *The Ferryboat Serenade*. Another pretty fourteen-year-old was Jean Bamforth, who did an acrobatic act— she now works in the Wardrobe Department of the BBC. There was Dorothy Duval, who did a big boot dance. It was quite something to see that little titch leap out from the wings straight into a big walloping routine. She is now married to Tommy Trinder's brother Fred. There was Vera Howe who sang *Alice Blue Gown*. There was Arthur Tolcher who played the harmonica. There was Stanley Ambler who sang *I'll Walk Beside You*.

A juvenile talent is a delicate flower. There was a regular turnover of pubescent boy sopranos whose voices tended to drop in mid-note. We saw a few run off the stage in tears. Apart from the shock and embarrassment, it usually meant for them the end of show business, or rather this honeymoon with show business.

We had our quota of 'older' discoveries—fellows in their twenties, like Eddie Gunter, who whistled *In a Monastery Garden*, and Frank Hines who did an impression of Charlie Chaplin with a spotlight flickering to make it look like an old silent film.

The regular pros on the bill were Alice and Rosie Lloyd, sisters of the famous Edwardian music hall star, Marie Lloyd, besides an attractive coloured American singer, Adelaide Hall. We had Tessie O'Shea on the bill quite a lot. Also June Marlowe, who sang with Jack Hylton's band and is now married to Joe Davis, the snooker player. We had a dance act, The Danny Lipton Trio and for comedians, Archie Glen, a double-act George Moon and Dick Bentley, and there was Dickie Hassett, a very perky Cockney, with his catch phrase of 'large lumps'. A gag of his was 'I don't have to worry about money. I have enough to last me for the rest of my life—if I drop dead at six o'clock tonight.' We still use it occasionally.

Another comic, who joined us shortly after we started our double-act, was a tough old codger called Scott Saunders. 'Hey, you two, that line in your act—"My wife was sent to me from heaven—as a punishment!" That's my gag,' he accused.

'Well,' we said, 'we pinched it off So and So.'

'All right, then. You can borrow it for this week,' he said.

'Thanks.'

We were relieved. It was one of our big laughs—two boys of fourteen with spots talking about their wives. But the very next time we used the gag it dropped dead. Not a titter from the audience. Later we discovered why. Scott Saunders had already got a laugh with it in the first half.

I'll say this for *Youth Takes a Bow*, it was an excellent grounding in professional theatre work. At one stage it was incorporated with Jack Warner's famous wartime show, *Garrison Theatre*, and we were called upon to help by playing various parts in his sketches. I'll never forget a kind of spectacular number called *Dancing Through the Ages*, in which I had to come on very doddery in a bald wig and dance *The Anniversary Waltz*. I was supposed to be ninety-seven.

ERNIE   And he looked it—even without make-up. What about the sketch in which I played the part of Jack Warner's wife's lover. She and I are kissing and cuddling when Jack and his little daughter arrive home unexpectedly. Lover hides in the cupboard just before they enter. Cupboard begins to shake.

Daughter   Daddy, there's a ghost in the cupboard.

Daddy (opening cupboard and seeing lover)   How dare you frighten my little girl like that.

ERIC   We toured the top variety circuits, travelling every Sunday on train journeys which remain in my memory as marathons of bum-numbing boredom. If you took a walk down one of those train corridors you might see discoveries' mums and various people on the bill gossiping or snoozing. There'd be Cyril Naylor, Mary's father, playing poker with the musicians—we saw men lose entire pay packets on a journey with the result that Ernie and I were put off gambling for life. And there'd be ourselves with the other kids eating sandwiches and drinking pop or running up and down the corridor and, when adult tempers became frayed, getting the odd thump and being told to get back inside.

That was the form so let's skip the next six months while *Youth Takes a Bow* tours wartime Britain and Ernie Wise manages more or less on his own. Then we get to Oxford where we are booked to appear at the New Theatre. The town is full of troops, Ernie is unlucky. He has trudged about in the blackout, knocking on doors. He is found, desolate, at ten that night by Doreen Stevens, a very sweet girl of eighteen, who used to sing in Maurice Winnick's Band and had joined the show a short while before. Meanwhile my mother and I are comfortably settled in at our own digs.

I can see it perfectly. A pleasant front room, a bed-sitter, or 'combined chat' as it was known, with a pot of aspidistras, a Stag at Bay on one wall, a flight of china ducks on another, a roaring coal fire, and a gasunda, a pot that goes under the bed.

Knock on the front door. My mother and I prick up our ears. Clock, clock, clock—footsteps in the hall below. Pause.

'Yes?'

'Excuse me. I'm Doreen Stevens. This is little Ernie Wise. Have you got any room in your house?'

'No, we're full up this week. We've got two or three people from the theatre, you see.'

'Well, little Ernie has been walking about for hours now, and I've tried too, and we can't get him fixed anywhere.'

So my mother says, 'Is it our Ernie?'

I looked round the door. 'I'm afraid so!!!!!' (Ernie, look—only five.)

'We can't let her turn the lad away,' my mother said. She went out on the landing, 'Hullo Doreen, hullo Ernie.'

'I don't know what we're going to do about him.' Doreen looked worried.

My mother said, 'Well, if you like, he can come in with us. I'll sleep in the single bed and the two boys can share the double.'

I was hoping Doreen was going to say Ernie could sleep at her place and she could share the double-bed with me. But she never did.

So Ernie joined us. Next day my mother opened her digs address book. She was about to write off for digs to the next stop, Newcastle.

She said, 'Ernie, would you like to come in with us? You can sleep with Eric. It will be a saving.'

Ernie jumped at it. We paid thirty shillings a week for my mother and maybe a pound for me, all in, which included full board and the roaring fire lit by the landlady or her daughter at eight o'clock while you still slept. Not only would it be cheaper for Ernie to come in with us, but he would be saved the trouble of having to do his own advance bookings, and he would be saving on the stamps. Since he and I would be sharing a bed it would be a saving for my mother too.

Money was tight enough. Out of what she had left from my five pounds a week after paying for our digs, she kept perhaps fifteen shillings for things like biscuits and cigarettes. I was given five shillings pocket money, and a pound went home to my father. Having Ernie to share was definitely a help. As for Ernie, he was well off. Out of his seven pounds a week, he sent three pounds ten shillings home. His board and shared bed with me cost him fifteen shillings, and the rest went into his hoard. 'Keep your hand on your bankbook,' his mother had instilled into him, 'it's your greatest friend.'

As Eric's mother was directly responsible for starting the double act, and indeed is the only one capable of an objective account of its birth pangs, let us go back to her at her home at Hestbank, in Morecambe Bay.

SADIE I became very fond of Ernie. He was such a nice, gentle boy.

ERIC Rubbish.

SADIE Will you be quiet. Ernie was gentle and shy, and sincere. Eric used to call him Lilywhite. 'Look at Lilywhite, he never puts a foot wrong,' he would say. He was right. Ernie never did wrong. Not that he was prim or prissy, or goody-goody, which is a person who just acts good but is really not good inside. Ernie was just naturally good, naturally truthful, fair and honest. We toured and lived together for years. I *know* Ernie.

On tour, when it came to the luggage, I would look around and there would be my son helping Mrs Bamforth and Jean, or some other pretty girl or her mother. I'd be furious with Eric, but Ernie would say, 'It's all right, I'm helping you.'

ERIC He was always a crawler.

36

SADIE You're not too big to hit. If I may continue, Ernie would never hear a word said against Eric, nor would he ever split on him. I remember when I first found out that Eric was smoking— I was turning out his pockets and came across a packet of cigarettes with some smelly butts.

'Come here, Ernie, I want you a minute,' I said. 'is Eric smoking?'

'Why don't you ask him?'

I said, 'Well I have but I can't get a proper answer. Anyway, I know he is.'

'Is he?'

'You know he is smoking.'

'Do I?'

I just could not get him to confirm or deny what I knew to be true.

Eric is very temperamental, which I call sheer bad temper. When they first started doing their double-act, they often used to alter their gags, but if Ernie made a slip on the stage Eric would go jumping mad.

'You're not a bit of good, Ernie. You're supposed to have learnt this.'

One day I was furious. 'Eric,' I said, 'don't you let me hear you speak like that to Ernie. Go straight upstairs.'

Eric stumped out of the room, his face scarlet with anger.

Ernie turned to me. 'You know, you shouldn't have interfered.'

'But I'm sticking up for you,' I said.

'Don't you see, Eric is only trying to make me the best feed in the country, like Jerry Desmonde is to Sid Field,' Ernie said.

'Make *you* the feed!'

'Yes, and shall I tell you something? He's going to be the best comic in the British Isles.'

Later I told Eric this, and there was no more temperament from my son, never another cross word, never any more argument. That's the honest truth.

When they first started the double-act, it was agreed that whatever was earned was split straight down the middle. They just shook hands over it and it didn't matter which of them got the

37

laughs. That holds today. No contract exists between them. Either could walk out tomorrow.

There is something between Eric and Ernie that no one will ever come between. It is what this new word empathy seems so perfectly to describe. It is a relationship which I think only two men are capable of having, men who have the complete faith and trust and understanding of each other. Eric and Ernie have got to the stage where they can practically read each other's thoughts. They have been together for so long and they are so much on the same wavelength and they know each other so intimately that each can, probably through instinct and habit, guess precisely how the other is going to react. At the start it was a question of their meeting somewhere halfway. For Ernie it meant having to convert from his fairly slick song and dance act to comedy, and for Eric it meant a change from his gormless comedy act to something really quite subtle.

The origin of the double-act was accidental. The three of us were living and touring together when the show reached Coventry, just a week after the town had been hit pretty badly in the bombing. We were in Birmingham during the week of the Coventry blitz. The digs we were going to in Coventry had been flattened, so we decided to stay on in Birmingham and commute the twenty-one miles to Coventry every day by train.

Well, have you ever tried travelling with two fifteen-year-old discoveries in a compartment in the blackout with both of them supercharged with adrenalin after a show? There wasn't a minute's peace for me. You couldn't talk sense to either of them but they would answer you back with some cheeky gag from one of the acts. They were forever taking people off in the show, particularly Moon and Bentley.

In sheer despair one night I said, 'Now look, instead of all this malarky, why don't you put your brains to some use? Try and do a double-act of your own. All you need are a few fresh jokes and a song.'

'That's an idea,' one of them said.

'Yes,' the other agreed. 'That's a very good idea.'

And immediately they got down to planning it.

I suggested a few gags. 'Oh, they're too old-fashioned,' they said.

'All right,' I said, 'you're so clever, you work on the gags. I'll talk to Alice and Rosie Lloyd about a song. You need a nice soft-shoe dance to finish on.'

Alice suggested *By the Light of the Silvery Moon*. The boys loved the idea. They worked out a dance routine and practised it till they had it well-nigh perfect. The gags weren't so easily come by. As far as I remember, they stole most of them from acts they had seen in the past, like the one in which Eric walks on the stage wearing an outsize hat with his hand inside the hat.

'What's the matter?' Ernie asks. 'Have you got a headache?'

'No,' says Eric, 'my hat's too big.'

One quality both of them possess, and it was evident right from the start, and that is professionalism. They always worked very hard. It was perfection or nothing. And, most important of all, they worked to a theme which has been steadily evolving along the years. The key to the act then was that it should be so barmy people would laugh. Eric runs on with a coat hanger.

Ernie What's that?
Eric A hanger.
Ernie What's it for?
Eric An aeroplane.

Originally they based their style on Abbott and Costello, even to the American accents, with Ernie as the straight man as he was the good-looking personality boy, and Eric as the comic, because he could look like a vacant American college dude in glasses and a big fedora hat.

Some of their gags, I am sure, they didn't even understand, like the one in which Eric comes mincing on with his hand on his hip.

Ernie What are you supposed to be?
Eric I'm a businessman.
Ernie A businessman doesn't walk like that.
Eric You don't know my business.

Anyhow, we lived, ate and slept the double-act. It took three or four weeks for the boys to get all this material together. It ran about four minutes. Bryan Michie liked it. 'Yes, very good,' he said, but he didn't say anything else.

39

'When can we do it in the show, Mr Michie?' Eric asked.

'I don't know. Mr Hylton would have to see it first.'

Poor Bryan Michie. He was a charming man, well-spoken and well-educated—he had been a schoolmaster—but he wasn't prepared to risk rocking the boat because the double-act could only go on the bill at the expense of some other child prodigy. The chance came when we got to Liverpool and Jack Hylton came up to see the show.

'Leave it to me, I'll tackle Mr Hylton,' Ernie said.

Not that he was cocksure; they were both too apprehensive and desperately wanting to do the double-act. After all their planning and rehearsing it was almost as if their lives depended on it.

Ernie waited for Jack Hylton to go into Bryan Michie's dressing room, then, after swallowing a couple of times, he knocked and went in.

'Oh hullo, Ernie, how are you getting on?'

'Fine, Mr Hylton. Yes, fine. By the way, we've got a little double-act together, Eric Bartholomew and I. Would you like to see it?'

'Certainly I will see it. Come along during the interval.'

So, during the interval, they did the double-act for the great man in Bryan Michie's dressing room.

Jack Hylton said, 'The act's not bad, but don't sing that bloody song.' Then, to Bryan Michie, 'Put it in on Friday night, and take out So and So.'

The boys were thrilled, but now we were stuck for a soft-shoe dance. Again I got together with Alice and Rosie. They suggested *Only a Bird in a Gilded Cage*. It suited the boys' dance routine perfectly.

When the time came for their debut together as a double-act, Jack Hylton and I were standing in the wings. We wished them luck. Then Bryan Michie walked out to introduce them, and they were on. None of us can remember the date except that it was a Friday night at the Liverpool Empire in 1941. But I can see the two of them there on the stage in the full glare of the lights, so very young but already such ardent and hard-working little troupers. The audience were loving them. I don't know what Jack Hylton was thinking, but I know I was in tears.

They got a marvellous reception. We were going on to Glasgow and you can imagine the thrill it was when Jack Hylton said they could do the double-act again for the whole of the Glasgow week in addition to their usual single acts.

ERNIE That was the start, but it took a while before our double-act became an established part of the bill. Bryan Michie had too tricky a course to steer through difficult shoals of parental rivalry to give us all the breaks we were begging for.

With Cyril Naylor at his elbow, helping with the clerical work, there was never any question about Mary's place in the batting order, which is not to say Mary wasn't deserving of it. Mary was; she was good. But for the rest Bryan had to contend, when we were at full strength, against such formidable claimants as Arthur Tolcher's mother, a pro of the old school, thoroughly versed in theatre lore and superstition; she would sit on a skip, a large wardrobe basket, in the wings, her legs never touching the ground, forever knitting. And Dorothy Duval's mother, Stanley Ambler's mother, Harry Bristow's mother, and Jean Bamforth's mother.

Every Monday morning at bandcall at the next theatre on the tour, Ernie and I would say, 'Mr Michie, can we do the double-act this week?'

'No, lads, I'm afraid not.'

A week later. 'Mr Michie . . .' and so it went on until he didn't have the heart to say no and he squeezed us in somehow. Or somebody's voice broke and we took his place until the next discovery on the list of those who had been auditioned was sent for.

An early problem was my stage name. Nobody liked Bartholomew and Wise. Bryan Michie wanted to call us Bartlett and Wise or Barlow and Wise. The matter was finally settled in Nottingham.

My mother was talking to Adelaide Hall, the coloured American singer on the bill, when her husband, Bert Hicks, came up.

My mother said, 'We're trying to think of a name for Eric.'

Bert was a big American Negro with a deep voice. He said, 'There's this friend of mine, a coloured boy who calls himself Rochester because he comes from Rochester, Minnesota. Where do you come from?'

'Morecambe.'

'That's a good name. Call him Morecambe.'

My mother liked it and I liked it, and from there on I was Morecambe on the bill.

We were in the rehearsal room where the preliminary stages of The Morecambe and Wise Show *are agonised into shape. It was a good place for Eric, Ernie and myself to get together because, once the others left, we had it to ourselves. Reminiscing together, the boys would prompt and spark each other off.*

ERNIE The next milestone was when Bryan Michie invested in some smart outfits for us. These were made-to-measure, and we appeared for the first time dressed alike in blue blazers, gaberdine trousers and the traditional straw hats. By that time several discoveries had left the show for one reason or another and I had tackled Jack Hylton about some extra money for the double-act. He gave us each a pound a week rise. By that time too we had added a song to the start of the act and a few more pirated gags. For example, Eric would come on with an apple on a string at the end of a stick. 'What are you doing?' I'd ask.

   Eric   I'm fishing.

   Ernie   Fishing? You don't catch fish with an apple. You catch fish with a worm.

   Eric   The worm's in the apple.

ERIC Well worth that extra pound a week!

ERNIE Our side-line was fire-watching. There was a rota with the names of all the men in the show who were over eighteen. Those on fire-watching duty had to spend the night in the theatre, and in the event of an air raid they went on the roof and put out any incendiaries that came their way. It was a bore being on the rota, especially for those who had a real interest in going to bed. So Eric and I, illegally because we were under age, took their places on the rota for a fee of half-a-crown a night each. Many were the nights we spent in empty theatres full of eerie creaks and strange draughts, with just one dim light on, scared to death, playing cards, with Eric nervously chain-smoking away his rota money.

ERIC While Lilywhite banked his.

ERNIE There was a blitz the night we were doing a half-crown rota in Chatham.

ERIC And I was so scared I couldn't have put out my cigarette much less an incendiary. Fortunately nothing, not even the ray of a searchlight, fell on our roof. There were a few more nights of jellied terror in Swansea and London. But apart from fire-watching there were terrors enough in ordinary human inter-course, by which I mean the everyday business of living, in our case on tour. Take Sheffield—and I wish somebody would! We arrived the day after a blitz and managed to find accommodation at an *Upstairs Downstairs* type of house where a rather intimida-ting, definitely-not-a-regular landlady took us in. The family were sleeping 'downstairs' and we had to go 'upstairs'. One of our bedroom walls had been hit—there was a hole in it opening on to the sky. We were frozen stiff with the cold, but—and I remember it clearly—the three of us were too scared to go down and ask her ladyship for another blanket.

ERNIE I remember in Sheffield we used to take the tram to the theatre, the Empire. We were doing two shows, at two o'clock and five-thirty because of the blitz. We liked that. It gave us the evening off.

ERIC By that time Bryan Michie's discoveries were reduced to Jean Bamforth, Ernie and myself. Ernie went on first and sang *Run Rabbit Run*. I followed with my *I'm Not All There*, after which Jean came on and did three or four minutes of acrobatics. Jean had a marvellous trick. She would lie on her tummy and arch her legs back to her head on which she would be balancing a glass of water, at the same time passing a hoop under herself. Ernie and I followed her with our double-act, and finally the three of us finished on a song called *The Waiter, the Porter and the Upstairs Maid*.

By now our double-act had reached seven minutes, or ten if we worked slowly. It was pure rubbish yet we were so confident of ourselves that when Bryan Michie finally disbanded the show in early 1942 we seriously considered launching ourselves in variety as true professionals. There were problems, however. The first was how to get started—at sixteen.

4

ERNIE   What appealed to Eric about variety was the fact that it was an easy life. Don't let anyone kid you that it was hard work. I know that dancers, acrobats, trapeze acts, wire acts, jugglers, magicians, contortionists, and other speciality acts did have to practise every day to keep their performance from falling off. But for the others, the comics especially, the job was a sort of habit.

The average comic made a career out of one act, but even the above average did not have that much more to offer. Take Jimmy James who was a great comic. Jimmy had perhaps four or five variations to his basic act in the whole of his working life, and that was really quite a repertoire. We knew acts who had gone on and on without a change for two decades, even longer; so much so they were virtually incapable of introducing a single new word. If you asked them to read something where they hadn't been used to reading anything, they were practically done for, as they would be too if you took away some familiar prop.

Dickie Henderson has a classic story about G. H. Elliott, 'the chocolate-coloured coon'. G.H. used to come out and say, 'Folks, I got a letter from my Lindy Lou.' Then he'd put his hand in his pocket, take out an envelope, open it and sing his famous song, reading the letter. G.H. had done the number for maybe forty years but he had never learnt the words. One night some joker in the show replaced the letter with a blank piece of paper. G.H.

44

opened it on the stage and promptly 'dried'. He couldn't remember a single word of the song.

ERIC Not only G. H. Elliott. I've got to have an 'idiot board' with the words of our song, *Bring Me Sunshine*, when we sing it on TV. I know them backwards—sometimes I sing them backwards—but I wouldn't feel secure without my prop.

ERNIE It's funny how the mind can get stuck in a sort of idea rut. Half the villains who get caught are copped because their 'trade mark' is known to the police: it was a bright idea once but they hadn't the wit to think of something else. It was like that with the old-time comics, and at one stage Eric and I were definitely heading that way. I remember once at the Lewisham Hippodrome we decided to introduce a new gag into the act. It took us at least four hours, in a café over a pot of tea, rehearsing a few new lines. It was almost traumatic.

The point I am trying to make is that at the start the idea of an easy life in variety appealed to Eric, though there were times, I remember, when he did seem to have some hang-up about not liking show business which, if psychoanalysed, could I'm sure be traced back to that gormless costume he had to wear in *I'm Not All There* until he was sixteen. That stuck in his craw because he thought it made the pretty young discoveries laugh at him, while I, he imagined, was absolutely devastating in my dress suit and straw hat.

Actually, for my part, I was not all that desperately interested in girls. I was too ambitious, too keen to get on in show business to devote much ardour to the chase. Besides, it had been drummed into my head by my mother to be wary of girls. 'Keep those scheming hussies at a distance,' she used to say. Eric's mother too was forever warning us. 'Marry a girl and your fourpenny pie will cost you eight pence.'

Until Eric and I teamed up, his mother was the driving force in his life. I took over from her.

ERIC How did we get on to this head-shrinking tack? Anyhow, the show finally came to an end at Swansea, and it happened rather suddenly after an air raid. Business hadn't been good for some time. Bryan Michie had been going around looking grim.

Then at last it came, a telegram from Jack Hylton instructing him to close, and that was it.

We held a council of war, my mother, Ernie and myself.

'We've got to do something,' I said. 'Let's head for London. We'll be snapped up.'

'Yes,' said Ernie. 'The agents will jump at us. We'll probably make thirty or forty quid a week joint.'

'Boys,' said my mother, 'it won't be as easy as that. Bryan Michie has explained the position. You are only employable as child discoveries, and there isn't another discovery show going.

'*Child discoveries!*' I quivered with indignation.

'Facts have to be faced,' she said.

'What does Bryan Michie know?' I said. 'We've knocked audiences out before, knocked them sideways. We'll do it again.

'Not at present,' my mother said firmly. 'We'll go back home to Morecambe, and Ernie will go back to Leeds. You can get yourselves jobs till you're both a little older.'

'Jobs!'

Neither of us had done an honest day's work in our lives. The very thought filled me with horror. I'm sure it was at that 'moment in time', as I have heard a Cabinet Minister put it, that I ceased resenting *I'm Not All There*. I would willingly have returned to it, and hung on to it, as G. H. Elliott had to Lindy Lou's letter, for forty years.

So I was dragged back to Morecambe where I was fed into Britain's industrial war machine, doing a ten-hour day in a local razor blade factory for seventeen shillings and sixpence a week.

Ernie, not being immediately under the thumb of a parent, thought he would go up to London to try his luck on his own. He stayed with a Japanese family of acrobats, but variety was practically at a standstill on account of the bombing. He was advised to go back home, which he did. Back in Leeds, he did a coal round with a friend's dad who had a horse and cart.

Miserable, frustrated, we kept in touch. After three months of 'real' work, Ernie came to stay with us in Morecambe. We thought we would have a shot at getting into a seaside concert party. We tried everywhere along that coast but never did make it in concert party even when every able-bodied male between eighteen and fifty who could stand had been called up.

ERNIE We went to my mother in Leeds and played some of the working men's clubs there and in Bradford where people remembered me as a kid with my father. But there were not many dates. It was a difficult time when I'm afraid I had to presume on my 'best friend', my bank book, by borrowing from it. Anyhow, the wonderful thing about being a double-act is that you are never out on your own in the cold, cold world. Problems are things you share while the plans you make have a sort of improved fail-safe mechanism because if one of you is off the mark, and we all are from time to time, the other is there as a check. In our case we also had Eric's mother who had faith in us, and against all advice and during the worst possible period she decided that her prodigies must come to London if they were ever to take the plunge into the world of professional variety. Was she crazy or inspired? Probably both, but she was wonderful too to have created such an unbelievable opportunity for us.

We found ourselves a flat at Mornington Crescent, near Euston, and went to see an agent in Charing Cross Road. We can't remember his name. All he said was, 'Why don't you go round to the Hippodrome on Monday? George Black is auditioning for his new show, *Strike a New Note*.

I'll not forget that audition. The place is now the Talk of the Town, London's top cabaret date, with tables where they serve dinner and drinks. Then it was a theatre with George Black sitting in the stalls, very opulent, with his two sons George and Alfred, and Paula, his very pretty daughter about our age. I had met them when I was staying with Jack Hylton's family at Angmering-on-Sea.

Eric and I watched the auditions before our turn. One artist sang a song, another did a bit of a tap dance, a third walked across the stage showing what she possessed fore and aft. George Black's assistant would say, 'Right. Leave your name and address.' Then, to the wings, 'Next.'

That sort of thing wasn't for us. We had brought all our props. We were going to knock George Black sideways. We gave him our full act, at nine minutes, and I'll say this for him, he politely

47

endured the agony. He went even further. Afterwards, in the wings, his assistant said, 'All right, get changed, and come down into the stalls. Mr Black would like to see you.'

We went through the pass door into the auditorium. George Black was charm itself.

'Hullo, Ernie. You all right? What sort of money have you two been getting?'

I then learnt my first lesson about money in show business. Thinking he'd be sorry for us and give us more, I said, 'Not much, Mr Black. We've never had more than £20 a week between us.'

Immediately he said, 'I'll give you that.'

Later the agent said, 'You idiot. You shouldn't have talked money. I could have got you another fiver. Perhaps even a tenner.'

The thought of it still makes me sick. But getting back to George Black. Emboldened by the fact that one of Britain's top showmen actually wanted us in his new show, I said, 'Whereabouts in the show will we do our act?'

George Black tugged at his collar. 'Well, you won't actually be doing your act in the show. You'll just be doing bits and pieces.'

It felt like a bucket of cold water. My smile had gone. I said, 'Mr Black, if you don't want our act, I don't think we are really interested.'

The thought of our colossal impudence at sixteen still makes me weak at the knees.

George Black smiled; he had great charm. 'Boys, I'll tell you what we can do. Our second comic is Alec Pleon. You can take his place if he is ever off for any reason. We need a strong stand-in act. It's an important position.'

'OK, Mr Black, that's very fair,' I said, placated and relieved.

For the next fourteen months that we were in his show together Eric and I prayed every day that Alec Pleon would fall ill, or take the wrong bus, or be arrested, or miss the show for any reason at all, but he turned out to be the fittest man in show business; he arrived at the theatre with the most depressing regularity. If he hadn't, for some inexplicable reason, missed two performances,

48

we would never have got our big break. On both occasions the audience simply stared at us, open-mouthed, aghast, wondering what was being inflicted on them and why.

'What fools!' we said of them. 'What has the blackout done to people's sense of humour? Have we lost the war or something?'

Anyhow, at least *we* loved our act, we thought it wonderful and were prepared to do it anywhere, anytime, at the drop of a hat. At the American officers' club in Hans Crescent, off the Brompton Road, we found a virtually captive audience. Mary Naylor used to perform there and come away with armfuls of goodies and we climbed on to her bandwagon. Though the Americans never applauded our act half as much as they did hers, we were given cigars, Chesterfield cigarettes, chewing gum, ice-cream.

One evening, the entertainments officer said, 'Say, you guys like pumpkin pie?'

'Pumpkin pie! Oh, gee, we love it,' we said, never having heard of pumpkin pie much less having tasted it. As it turned out this classic Mid-Western dish wasn't bad at all, though psychologically I'm sure it would not have been possible for us not to have liked pumpkin pie. For we lived an American fantasy, sang American songs, used American expressions, spoke with American accents.

As it happened, *Strike a New Note* was a smash hit, and therefore a wonderful show to be in, full of new ideas and new, exciting stars. Sid Field, who had been touring the provinces for years, unknown except to Northern audiences, was famous the day after the show opened in London, with Jerry Desmonde famous too as his feed. Zoë Gail, the South African musical comedy star, was the leading lady, and they were supported by Derek Roy, Bernard Hunter and some of the most beautiful girls I have ever seen.

The Morecambe and Wise 'bits and pieces' were cut one after another, leaving just me doing an impression of James Cagney singing *Yankee Doodle Dandy* for which Adolphe Menjou, the Hollywood film actor, personally congratulated me one night after the show. We soon settled down to being what we really were, just glorified chorus boys, though we kidded ourselves we were on a higher level. One night, Charles Henry, the stage director, announced that all the principals were requested to go into the bar where Mr George Black had something to say to them.

What were we? I looked at Eric. He didn't know.

I thought I'd better ask. 'Mr Henry, are we principals?'

'I don't know, boys,' he said. 'But to be on the safe side, better stay with the chorus.'

ERIC Mind you, that was never a hardship. Those girls! Their dressing room was right on top. I don't know whether they thought Ernie and I had been neutered, or were too young, but they never bothered to cover themselves whenever we went upstairs to see them which was pretty often. You'd come across girls stark naked—sorry, sometimes in black shoes and black gloves dressed as the five of Spades.

Ernie and I, and another glorified chorus boy called Billy Dainty, had a tiny dressing room up near the top. Opposite our door was a dirty little window which overlooked several bedrooms of the Mapleton Hotel. It was a place the American soldiery used for what they called an afternoon shack-up. That window became a magnet. There were days when the entire cast of *Strike a New Note* would be at the window watching the bedroom Olympics. Faces were tied to the window like fish by their gills, with other faces behind them desperately awaiting their turn, maddened by the applause.

ERNIE You're wrong when you say 'the entire cast'. I for one never got my eye to that window.

ERIC Of course not, you weren't tall enough.

ERNIE I'll ignore that. To get back to the show. That whole experience of being in it, opened a fantastic new world to us. We saw famous people in the audience who later came backstage—Clark Gable, James Stewart, George Raft, Deborah Kerr who came with the film producer Alfred Hitchcock, Gabriel Pascal, and many, many others. The show had a certain cachet: everybody who came to London had to see it. Even *The Man Who Never Was*. This was a dead body that the Allies planted on the Germans with false identity papers in the hope they would send back in his place a spy who would lead them to other German spies in Britain. Which was what happened. In the dead body's pocket were two ticket stubs from *Strike a New Note*.

For the first time in our lives we had a glimpse of West End night life. Girls in the show with rich daddies—and some were merely playing at show business as part of their war effort—invited us to stately homes in the country for the week-end. We were invited to Paula Black's birthday party at the Bagatelle Nightclub—if you had asked me to describe my idea of Shangri La, I would have said, 'Have you ever been to the Bagatelle?' Wendy Toye, the show's dance director, would take us back to her house in London for drinks and we'd meet West End stars. We went to parties at Derek Roy's flat where we were shown his unbelievable wardrobe of suits. We might spend a Sunday at the Enfield home of a young dancer in the show called Johnny Brandon. Johnny used to try to speak like Mickey Rooney.

'Hi there, Pop. Can I borrow the Jag?'

'Certainly.'

Pop would throw him the keys of the Jaguar, and we'd drive about thirty yards to the shop at the corner where they sold sweets and newspapers. We'd drive back the thirty yards and spend the afternoon playing records or living a show business fantasy in which we wrote ourselves fabulous American radio scripts.

ERIC By now, I was taller than Ernie, and I had lost what used to be described as my 'poorly look' and is commonly and I am sure mistakenly associated with a certain form of doom. I had shed my *I'm Not All There* costume for good and all. I was virile. At the window I had learnt all about the birds and the bees, and there was a girl called Gloria Gold, aged fifteen, whom I had once taken to a film in the West End. Then another girl, Prudence James, caught my fancy. I took her to the Pavilion to see *The Cat and the Canary*—there wasn't much else one could do on £1 a week pocket money. The third big romantic episode of that fourteen-month period was when Ernie and I went on a Sunday from Upper Tooting, where we lived in a rented house under my mother's watchful eye, to Piccadilly, met a singer in the show called Cherry Lynn and we went to a Chinese restaurant. She paid.

The chapter would not be complete if I did not mention our

radio series, *Youth Must Have Its Fling*, on the Light Programme of the BBC. They had wanted Sid Field. Sid wasn't interested; he was more of a visual comedian. We were thrilled to stand in, and a number of boys and girls from *Strike a New Note* would come up to the Aeolian Hall in Bond Street to make up a studio audience. They did their best for us; overdid it if anything. Here's a clip from a Morecambe newspaper:

'Eric Bartholomew, sixteen years old, only son of Mr and Mrs George Bartholomew, of 43, Christie Avenue, known professionally as Eric Morecambe, perhaps the youngest comedian on the stage, broadcast with his partner, Ernie Wise, aged seventeen, of Leeds, on Tuesday evening in the feature, *Youth Must Have Its Fling*.

'They told jokes in the American style. Ernie was supposed to do the "feeding" but Eric complained that he took the laughs! The entire feature would have been much improved if the laughs of the young people forming the studio audience had been more spontaneous and not so obviously made to order.'

Then Ernie turned eighteen and got called up. He had the option of going into the Army, down the mines, or volunteering for the Merchant Navy. There was more money in the Merchant Navy so he plumped for that. Besides, he thought, Ah, opportunity knocks. I will get on a big boat to the States or Australia and see a bit of the world. In fact he wound up on a coaster. He rose to engineers' cook-steward, it took him two years to get over being seasick, and the nearest he got to action was seeing a knife fight in Gateshead.

ERNIE Calumny. I worked for the Gas Light and Coke Company, doing an unromantic but nevertheless vital job, bringing coals from Newcastle and South Shields down to London where we discharged at the Battersea Power Station.

We were engaged on a very strange contract—I never knew how it worked—known as the North Sea Coast Agreement, whereby we always did a quick turn around in London and had our time off on Tyneside where most of the crew lived. If coal supplies were held up, as often they were, we might have several days off. These I would spend either in Leeds or with Eric's parents in Morecambe. There were other breaks. You signed on with a crew for six months. Between boats your name went into a pool of seamen—you could be in it six or seven weeks on full pay, and during these periods I used to tour with Bryan Michie who had started another discoveries show. He paid me £10 a week.

ERIC I stayed on in *Strike a New Note* but not for long as the show broke up shortly after Ernie left.

ERNIE I was sorry I couldn't stay and hold the show together, but there was my war effort, of course.

ERIC Of course.

ERNIE The country's back was to the wall.

ERIC And Battersea needed coal—which I too was to be called on to provide. But hang on. I wasn't due for call up until May 1944, so in the meantime I got a job in ENSA as straight man to a Blackpool comic named Gus Morris. Gus had won the Military Medal in World War I. He had been wounded by a burst of machine-gun fire. He couldn't bend his right knee, and his left he could bend only half way, and he had only one eye, but he was a very funny man and very kind to me.

I remember he and I were at St Helens. The following week we weren't working, so I went home on the Saturday night after the show. On the Monday came a notice in the post for me to report to the labour exchange. I went down there and took my place in the queue.

'Bartholomew?'

'Yes.'

'Hullo, Eric, how are you?' said the man at the desk whom I knew.

'Fine,' I told him.

'Matter of fact, the doctor thinks so too. Your medical report says you're A1, and you're one of the chosen few who are going down the mines.'

'When?'

'Wednesday. New Town Colliery, Manchester. Take this voucher with you. We've fixed digs for you. At the depot there they'll issue you with your cap lamp, tin helmet and boots with toe-caps.'

In Manchester they said, 'You can either stay here or volunteer for any other mine in this area.'

Now my father had worked as a collier after World War I. 'I was down the mine at Accrington. You have relatives there. Volunteer for Acrington,' he advised.

So I did, to find that the mine had been condemned twenty years before. The conditions were terrible.

ERNIE Now do you see why I never let him handle the business side?

ERIC Some of the seams were literally no more than two feet high. Before this I had never carried anything heavier than a set of band books ——

ERNIE Band books! He never carried the band books—it would have been too much like tempting Providence to have let him. I carried the band books.

ERIC All right, he carried the band books. What I am trying to say is that I was not a weight lifter. What's more, I was a non-weight lifter, in delicate health and looking poorly, having to push great big tubs of coal along rails down pitch black tunnels with only a swinging Davey safety lamp of, I should guess, one candle-power. You had only to knock your lamp against a tub for it to go out.

'Fireman!' you called in a piping little voice that went in a quavering echo along the pit, and you'd wait perhaps twenty minutes for the fireman to come up to re-light it. I lived above a shop at Clayton le Moor with a couple, Mr and Mrs Birdikin, who owned the shop. Mr Birdikin had been a miner, his face tattooed blue with coal dust under the skin, his lungs brittle with silicosis. He would shake me awake at 5.30 in the morning. 'Come on, lad. Time to get up.'

I would go downstairs to a smell that has always nauseated me —frying bacon and eggs. They'd make me eat a hearty breakfast, and I'd step into the street with my bait, my mid-morning meal, tied in a red handkerchief—a round bun with a lump of cheese and a bottle of cold tea.

I lived for the week-ends at Morecambe where Ernie might turn up with a lump of boiling bacon or silverside which he had purloined from his ship's engineers.

I honestly don't remember seeing the pavements dry in Accrington. I had gone down the mine in A1 condition. In eleven months I was classified C3 and sent home with a touch of heart trouble to my mother's fussing which I enjoyed.

When I felt better, I went back to the razor blade factory for a spell, till my mother's eagle eye, scanning the 'Wanted' columns in *The Stage*, found that a touring show were looking for a straight man for their comedian, Billy Revel. I got the job, on £12 a week. The show ran for six months. After that my mother thought she'd better start looking again in *The Stage*.

She turned to my father. 'Look at this,' she said. 'The circus owner, Lord John Sanger, has hit on this bright idea of combining variety and circus. They are to tour the country in caravans, putting up the big top on village greens and in big towns and giving a show that will be a combination of the two different forms of entertainment. They are looking for a comic. I think I'll take Eric down to London to see them.'

Whatever my mother said went with my father and me. No question about that. We went to London. We met Edward Sanger, Lord John's brother, whom we had known previously as Bryan Michie's manager.

'As it happens, we have just engaged a comic,' he said. 'But you can be his feed. £10 a week?'

'OK,' we said.

'Great, great.'

'Whose the comic?' I asked.

He said, 'You will remember him—Ernie Wise.'

'Ernie Wise!' my mother repeated. 'B-but Ernie has always fed my son.'

'Not in our show,' Edward Sanger said. 'Ernie is the comic, Eric is the feed.'

'You're going against nature,' said my mother. 'My son'— her breast swelled—'has a certain something.'

'I know, but in this show he's the feed. It's already been settled. Ernie's on £12.'

5

Eric We received a letter from a woman the other day who asked whether it was really us she saw in Bodmin just after the war. 'But I could have sworn it was in a circus,' she added incredulously. Her voice (in the letter) took on a sweet, motherly note. 'What stands out in my memory is that one of you had such a nice smile.'

Ernie She was referring, of course, to me.

Eric His smile was unforgettable because, as the comic, he was getting £2 a week more than me, as feed.

Ernie Sanger's idea was a novel one. It was to combine two worlds of show business and take it to places where the occasional visit of the big top was the only form of entertainment. We had a tent which covered half an acre with a stage instead of a ring and seating for 700.

The entertainment was provided by a clown called Speedy Yelding, who also did a tightrope act and a whip act dressed as a cowboy; a man called Wally Lucken with a dog act; a band consisting of a pianist, a drummer and a banjo player; a singer called Molly Seddon, who had been on the BBC; a menagerie that you could walk around for sixpence. For a shilling you could be in it! It consisted of a donkey, a ring-tailed llama, a parrot, some hamsters, and a wallaby; and four dancing girls—Betty, who married one of the tent boys, Olga, who married an Irishman, Doreen, who in the fullness of time married me, and Rose, who didn't marry Eric; and last, and least, the two of us.

The whole thing was put together by a Welsh concert party producer who provided the jokes and sketches for Eric and myself. Some of the jokes were so obscure that I still haven't worked them out.

If the original idea was good, it was killed by the belief that country people were so starved of entertainment that they would accept any rubbish. The show was so bad that there were nights when the tent would rise up like a canvas mushroom and we would be waiting in full evening dress and Wellington boots (because of the mud), but literally nobody came.

ERIC One night we went through the entire performance for six kids who came in at half-price and were shown up to the cheapest seats at the back.

Inevitably came the crunch. We were all invited into Lord John Sanger's beautiful caravan. He was a big, bluff, extremely powerful man in his late forties who could break walnuts with his bare hands on the top of an iron tent peg and lift things like sixteen folding seats at one go to show us how to get cracking. We were expected to load and unload the seating. He was in gentleman-farmer tweeds. His wife was there, smiling.

'It's a simple matter,' he said. 'You all know the position. Either you take a cut, half the money you're getting, or we close.'

There was no argument. We were also called upon to help with more manual work though Eric drew the line when asked to walk the donkey along the sands at Weymouth with placards stuck on its backside, and was thereafter derisively termed 'gypped', meaning he had chickened out of a legitimate chore, something definitely not done in the circus fraternity.

ERIC The truth is I just hadn't sawdust in my blood or, I hope, my head. I did not respond, as some pretended to respond to the call of the road. I saw nothing romantic about having to use what I preferred to call our 'inconvenience'—a nauseous hole in the ground with a flimsy screen around it and a warning cough to ward off approaching footsteps. Once, when some mentally twisted practical joker sabotaged our sphincter-control by mixing Epsom salts with the sugar, delicacy had to be thrown to the winds. On the road that day, members of the company would suddenly bang on the driving cab of a vehicle for the driver to stop so that they could jump out and dive behind the nearest bush. In one emergency I had to go behind a hedge, in somebody's front garden, in full view of the house.

ERNIE And it was 14 May 1947, the poor lad's twenty-first birthday.

ERIC Life on the road was all right for people like Lord John Sanger with his enormous caravan with its ornate brass fittings and sideboard covered with carved silver animals and birds. Or even for the less exalted of the fraternity with smaller caravans; one was so small it shook violently during the inmates' love play. But we 'flatties' (outsiders) lived in extreme discomfort in converted RAF trailers and no facilities for washing except a canvas bucket.

Ernie and I shared one of these trailers with the band, in particular the pianist, Anton Petrov, a tall, thin man with a shock of bushy black hair, an impassive face, and a pipe. I cannot remember him without the pipe. He even smoked it while shaving, and in the confined space of the trailer in which we were crowded on narrow bunks we constantly breathed a blue fog.

ERNIE The best laughs were off the stage—like the time the trailer in which Eric was playing cards with Jock the drummer came unhitched going up a hill, rolled backwards and turned over in a ditch. There was Eric crying out pitifully, 'Help! My legs! I'm bleeding to death!' When we pulled him out he wasn't scratched, but his legs were covered with meths.

ERIC A great joke all round, but a mishap no one laughed about was when the mess bus also wound up in a ditch. This astonishing vehicle was a converted London Transport double-decker bus with the kitchen and larder occupying the lower deck while the upper deck was the mess. The cook was also the driver. After the accident, neither he nor his no-star restaurant were ever seen again. The job was taken on by Anton, who did the cooking, and Ernie who did the shopping. Ern was given a bike, a shopping bag, our ration books and of course the money which had to be extracted from Lord John Sanger.

The cooking was done over camp fires but there was nothing of a picnic atmosphere about it. We just collected dollops of Anton's terrible concoctions on tin plates and found somewhere to sit and not eat it. Everyone complained, so much so that eventually Anton, an artist subject to impassioned outbursts, got the message and flew off the handle. I cannot help feeling that the Epsom salts incident was a sample of his explosive revenge. I am still haunted by a grin of grim satisfaction around the stem of a briar pipe that itself was like a smouldering inverted question mark.

Anton had a single-barrel 12-bore hammer shotgun that he travelled with between his knees to pick off the odd pheasant which crossed our trail as we slowly wormed our way up and down the country roads of southern Britain.

Occasionally, on fortunate days, instead of cooking for us, Anton would be sent on ahead in what was called our scout car to book a meal for the company at a small, cheap, country cafe. One day, on a journey through Cornwall, he stopped at a place run by a Cornish old dear. Anton had considerable charm when he chose to remove the pipe and exert it.

'Madam,' and he flashed his best lady-killing smile, 'Good-morning. A lovely day, is it not?'

'It is indeed,' the old dear quavered.

'May I give you a piece of advance intimation? Do you know that *Lord John Sanger's Circus and Variety* will be arriving in two hours with thirty people starving for lunch? Now what can you serve and for how much?'

'Well,' she said, 'I can do you thirty Cornish pasties with mashed potatoes and greens.'

'Madam, that would be perfect.'

The charge was agreed, and Anton went back to find and guide us to this little oasis of hope. He hove in sight, reversed and took his place at the head of the convoy of bright yellow vehicles with bright red Edwardian lettering across the sides. Unfortunately Anton took a wrong turning and lost us our way. I am afraid the old dear is still waiting for *Lord John Sanger's Circus and Variety*.

ERNIE One of our big problems on the road was laundry. I would have been in a real fix had it not been for one of the dancers,

Doreen Blythe. Doreen came from Peterborough, in Northampton-shire. She had been to a ballet school and had danced as most ballet school pupils do, in pantomimes and musicals when these visited her home town. Later she went with a troupe of juvenile dancers to perform in a pantomime in Torquay. There she met a Scarborough girl, and at fifteen Doreen toured with this girl and two others in a dance act. Then, at sixteen, she had somehow got round her parents—she is an only child—to let her join *Lord John Sanger's Circus and Variety*.

I met her at Horley, in Surrey, where we foregathered before the tour began. I remember we were all having lunch at a café. I was sitting opposite her at a table, being my usual cheeky, forward self to cover up the nervousness I felt inside. We were having soup and I was trying to make a joke about how you could eat it with a posh or a not-so-posh accent. She was doing it very quietly indeed, but once, only once, she made a very slight sucking noise during a momentary silence. The others laughed but Doreen, only sixteen, reddened to the roots and looked supercilious daggers at me. I think I fancied her from that second. She was wearing a light-coloured suit which set off her lovely tan. I tried to strike up a conversation, but was ignored. After the meal she stumped off with her friend Rose. Rose now lives in Hull.

Over the next few days, Doreen kept trying to avoid me, but it was difficult because after all we were having to do quite a lot of rehearsing together and, remember, I was the principal comedian.

Eric and I took to stalking Doreen and Rose in the streets of Horley. They would see us coming and dive off down a side passage. Seldom have hunters made better use of cover and dead ground. In the end we trapped them in the doorway of a shoe shop with the display windows on either side. There was no dignified escape, and we managed to talk them into coming to a film.

It was *Hungry Hill*, starring Margaret Lockwood. All I remem-ber of it was that somebody kept bursting into the house and shouting, 'There's trouble at the mill', and that became a sort of running joke with us. Meanwhile Eric was hitting it off very well with Rose, and the upshot was that Doreen offered to do my

Comic (ha ha) and feed (guess who) soon after we teamed up in 1940

'Let's Have a Tiddly at the Milk Bar'

Overnight West End star in Jack Hylton's show, *Band Waggon*,
at the Prince's Theatre, with discoverer, Bryan Michie, and Doreen
Stevens

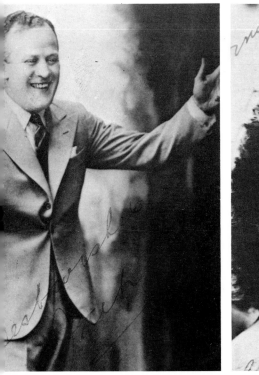

Jack Hylton, a 'typical Lancashireman', and his sister Dolly, who
toured with the show

Morecambe and Mother, an earlier double-act

Poor little poor boy (Wise, with wallet, in check suit) in *The Nignog Revue* at the Bradford Alhambra in 1936

Above left: Mother and Morecambe (*right*) the year he danced on his bottom. The other handful is Cousin George
Above right: Bert Carson and his Little Wonder with Connie who started the act

'Have ukes will travel'—and by golly you did when you heard them. Eric with George and Sadie in 1932

'Dorchester Follies'

YOUTH TAKES MICHIE AT ST GIVE

BORN WITH A SILVER CROON IN HER MOUTH — DOLLY ELSIE

THE DORMONDES IN THEIR SPILLING BEE

ERNIE WISE, THE JACK BUCHANAN OF TO-MORROW

FREDDIE BAMBERGER PIANOLOGUIST

GLORIA BRENT

EVERYBODY'S MAURICE-DANCING NOW— TO MAURICE WINNICK, OF COURSE

EDNA KAYE

GOIN ON BEND IS JE BAMFO

JACK HYLTON PRESENTS THE SHO AND CLEVER HAROL BERENS COMPERES JACK KNOWS HIS BERENS ALL RIGH

ARTHUR FERRIER 40

Bryan Michie's Discoveries in another guise

Will the real Ernie Wise please stand up

Adelaide Hall whose husband
suggested Eric's name

Doreen Stevens who brought us
together at Oxford

Sea Cook third class

laundry and Rose Eric's. We chalked that up as our first real success with the girls. We reckoned it must have taken real love to tackle our underwear on that tour.

Lord John Sanger's Circus and Variety finally ended up at the famous Nottingham Goose Fair in the first week of October. We were told we would have to work very hard for the three days of the fair. The tent was converted into a large booth without seats, and we had to take turns at spieling on a platform outside the tent. The audience were on a sort of conveyor belt, coming in at one side and shuffling along, urged on by great tough tent boys, while those on the stage kept up a continuous performance. On the first day, the Thursday, we did seventeen shows, on the second twenty-four shows, and on the Saturday we hit the record with thirty-two shows. After that we broke up, our voices gone, and went our separate ways.

It would be apposite here to introduce an ornithological note on the Wooslem Bird, otherwise known as the Wanga-Wanga Bird. This strange species first made its appearance with the emergence during the war of that curious human syndrome, the non-job. The Wooslem was observed as being parasitic upon it, a creature possessed of its own dynamic, ever-flurried, ever totally preoccupied, ever pursuing itself in ever-decreasing circles until it achieves the ultimately impossible disappearing trick. After the war, with the advent of television into the every-day lives of populations, the Wooslem Bird underwent a curious evolutionary change. It homed in on and attached itself to a phenomenon of this the greatest of the mass media. Akin in many ways to the Honey Guide of Africa, the Wooslem Bird led its followers to an object they sought, but this as explained was totally involuted, the most elusive and least tangible of all abstractions—success. Eric and Ernie too had heard the Wooslem's insistent call. By the time they returned to London in November 1947, it was already circling overhead. Its gyrations had begun.

*   *   *   *   *

ERIC My mother and I found digs with a Mrs Duer at 13, Clifton Gardens, Chiswick. The idea was that I should break into variety and she and Ernie shared the belief that I possessed some gifts as a comic. Also, I am sure, she had seen no hope at all for me at anything else. For her only child it looked like variety or the dole.

I am not addicted to any great belief in fate but I do think there is something in the law of averages. I am also prepared to subscribe to the fact that whether we like it or not chance plays a certain part in our affairs. A few days after my mother and I were installed at Chiswick we were walking in Regent Street, near Oxford Circus, when I looked across the traffic to see Ernie waving frantically from the other pavement. He dashed across. We fell about.

'Well, what do you know! Where are you staying, Ernie?'

'At Brixton, with Kura, one of The Iizuka Brothers.' They were his Japanese acrobatic friends who became The Java Brothers after Pearl Harbour. 'Where are you?' he asked. 'We're in Chiswick with a Mrs Duer. Very good digs. Thirty bob all in.'

'That's cheap. So I'll come over there, then?' Ernie said.

'Yes,' said my mother. 'You two might as well be out of work together as separately.'

Ernie moved in with us at Mrs Duer's and we decided, again at my mother's suggestion, to team up once more as a double-act and to build on to what we had had before when we were in Bryan Michie's Discoveries. We added some more stolen corn.

Example. I come on the stage with a vase on my shoulder.

Ernie What's that?
Eric A Greek urn.
Ernie What's a Greek earn?
Eric Thirty bob a week.

We put in an up-to-date opening song and a fresh soft-shoe number at the end. We had about ten minutes. Now it was time we found ourselves an agent.

For the reader who has never been through it, let me describe this the most depressing experience for the young artist trying to break into show business. Let us begin with the boy or girl with talent. Hollywood has brain-washed the youngster with miles of celluloid hocum about dedicated talent scouts whose devotion to their discoveries has brought joy to millions. We too believed this fairy tale, and I remember our seriously considering who we should choose for the privilege of handling our future career. It was quite a problem. We wanted a good man but at the same time we wanted to be fair, there being not a flicker of doubt in our minds that the moment we placed ourselves on the market they would rush at us like rickshaw coolies clamouring for our custom. We were quickly disillusioned. We couldn't get near enough to an agent to speak to one.

You would enter a tiny office in Charing Cross Road. A hatch would open. A secretary's face would appear.

'Yes?'

'We're a double-act. We would like Mr So and So to handle our bookings.'

'Where can we see you? Where are you working?'

'That's why we've come to you. We would like you to get us work.'

'We can't do that until we see you.'

It was ridiculous and heartbreaking. Gradually our eyes were opened. We came to learn that it was a common experience for most acolytes in our vulnerable position. We discovered too that most variety agents of that period had started in show business as bad acts and had turned to agency because they had come to terms with themselves. They had realised they could not survive as pros so they would survive on pros. As such they waxed fat and powerful, compensating themselves by despising and misusing the talent they knew they did not possess themselves.

Out-of-work variety acts would converge on an Express Dairy café that used to be near the Leicester Square tube station. The place would be packed with pros sitting over cups of morning coffee, from about ten till four, all saying how well they were doing and how this agent or that had a marvellous job lined up for them. Everything seemed to depend on the agent, who must be wooed and placated, whereas to my way of thinking it should be the other way about.

ERNIE Once we were conned by an agent. This was later when we were beginning to get established and a theatre manager wanted us on his bill. He rang this agent, thinking we were on his books. The agent was offered a 3-year contract for £100 a week rising to £120. Instead of admitting that he did not represent us, the agent

63

promptly got in touch with our agent and said, 'Look, I want the boys on a 3-year contract and will give them £80 a week rising to £100 a week.'

This was better money than we were getting at the time, and our agent clinched the deal. We found out about the real offer only by accident, but not before we were swindled out of over a £100.

ERIC I have never carried a torch for agents. In our early days there were many more than there are now, but none of them ever bothered to do anything about us until we managed to get a booking for ourselves and appeared on a stage. We have since had three agents whom we liked as people. Each was an exception to the rule. Our present agent, Billy Marsh, I consider one of the greatest show business agents in the world—he is in a unique position because of his worldwide contacts which he has worked hard to maintain. But in the winter of 1947, when our need was greatest, not one of them wanted to know and we tried every agent in the book.

I realise now that we had nothing even vaguely approaching a professional act. At the same time even if we had had the finest act in the world we couldn't have got it shown because we couldn't get a booking.

One way to find an agent was to get on a bill at the Met, the Metropolitan, Edgware Road, London's top variety show date, the artists' shop window, where agents would come to spot new talent. But we couldn't do that until we got an agent to book us at the Met, which brought us back to square one. The agents had it all nicely tied up between themselves. There were other show dates, the Brixton Empress, the East Ham Palace and the Chelsea Palace.

We tried the bookers direct but it was tough going. Here and there we picked up a date. I remember we got a fiver for doing a Masonic dance. There was £14 for a week in Bournemouth, and £25 for a very rough week at a place near the Barry Docks, Cardiff. The only real variety date we managed to land for ourselves during this dreary period was at the Palace, Walthamstow for the week of Monday 8 March 1948, with Harry Parry's Jazz Sextette at the top of the bill. One of the acts was Vic Wise and

Nita Lane ('the weak guy and his weakness') so we were billed as Morecambe and Wisdom. We made virtually no impression on the audiences, and the booker for that theatre dropped us.

ERNIE We again tried to get into concert party because we thought it would be a useful experience. We gave auditions to several well-known concert party producers but we were never quite sure what they wanted. Concert party requires a special, highly personalised style in which the performer must establish an immediate rapport with the audience. He has to be able to go on the stage and talk about anything and everything, making people laugh about local things and homely things. He must spark with and off the audience, as Arthur Askey could do so brilliantly, and more recently people like Bruce Forsyth, Des O'Connor (who incidentally got his experience as a Redcoat with Butlins) and of course Leslie Crowther. With our stage training we weren't able to free ourselves from the inhibition of a stage manager's stopwatch.

We got some work with ENSA. We also did a tour of the American army camps in Germany with Vic Lewis' Orchestra. We have heard horrifying stories of how British and Irish artists were treated by American military audiences. Val Doonican had a particularly bad time. I remember his telling us how at one American base he had to do his act on a stage between two TV sets, each on a different channel, with the sound blaring and the audience ignoring him completely. As it happened we went down quite well with American army audiences, possibly because they thought we were Americans.

ERIC So much has happened to us since that period that we tend not to think about it. Prefer not to, if you like, for the memory of it is still uncomfortable. It wasn't only a difficult time, it was frightening. We had to make it in show business because the alternative, 'real' work, didn't bear thinking about. My mother had gone back to Morecambe so we were without our morale prop though it must have been a comfort for her, I'm sure, to know we were in Mrs Duer's care. There were stretches of fourteen to eighteen weeks at a time when we were out of work and Mrs Duer kept us—'Pay me when you can, love.' The food was always good and for the money she also fed my dog. We were with her fourteen months. We would be painting too rosy a picture if we claimed we worked for even six weeks of that time.

Nell Duer was a tall, strong, angular woman, with a sharp finger she'd prod you with to hold your attention—I still have the dents. But she was always smiling—I don't remember an unpleasant word or incident in all the time we stayed with her. I called to see her a couple of years ago. She was exactly the same.

Mr Duer was his wife's physical opposite—small and slight. They had a son called John, who had a friend called John whom we called Ginger John to distinguish him. Both boys were mad on flying. John, we later heard, was turned down when he tried to become a pilot because of bad eyesight, but a couple of years ago, Ernie and his wife Doreen were flying to Malta where they own a flat. Who should be piloting the plane but Ginger John.

It's funny how certain memories remain. Mrs Duer's husband had a motorcycle. He would take us out for spins with Ernie in the sidecar and me on the pillion.

ERNIE For some reason we always seemed to go to Runnymede.

ERIC It was the only place the motorcycle knew.

ERNIE Being near Chiswick Empire, Mrs Duer accommodated a succession of variety acts; and, whenever paying guests (by that I mean guests who paid) arrived, Eric and I would vacate the front room we normally occupied, and our 'guest' chairs by the fire, and muck in with the family.

I remember we had Wilson, Kepple and Betty. Wilson and Kepple were two dancers, both thin as skeletons, who did an extremely funny dance without uttering a word on the stage. In the thirty years they had done their act together there had been a score of Bettys, but the routine had never altered a beat. They had always made good money and never seemed to spend much. They must have left a fortune.

Another act who used to stay at Mrs Duer's were Paul Kafka and his two assistants whose job was to stretch a wire between them, holding it in their teeth by biting on leather grips, while he performed on it. Paul was American—there were lots of good American acts touring Britain at the time. Variety was thriving in the boom that all forms of theatrical entertainment enjoyed immediately after the war. The trouble, as we soon found, was that there just weren't enough top-of-the-bill attractions to draw variety audiences and as a substitute managements started introducing nudes. By today's standards these were about as sexy as a Greek marble nymph—nudes weren't allowed to move on the stage. There'd be vigilantes from watchdog committees standing by to report if one of these human statues with goose pimples so much as sneezed. But it was enough to start discouraging the family audiences which had been the backbone of variety since Dan Leno was a boy. It was of course the beginning of the end.

How did we make out? I survived on my savings from which I drew out perhaps £2 a week and Sadie would send Eric about the same amount. From time to time we would take an overnight bus to Morecambe—the journey in those days lasted eleven hours. We would stay with Eric's parents for a week or fortnight, till we felt it was time we started trying again, and they'd send us back with a couple of extra quid in our pockets.

Fun? Well, we just couldn't afford any. Neither of us drank—our parents had brought us up to avoid pubs. Girls? Most of our mashing had been done on pocket money with usually the girls' mothers hovering in the background like dragons in a pantomime. True, there had been romance in circus and variety—I still wrote to Doreen. But at twenty-three with only six weeks' work in fourteen months, and only half of what came in from that as my share, there wasn't much to offer any girl.

Oddly enough, at no time in that desert of our lives did either of us ever think of making a spot of money in any way outside show business. Even at odd, temporary jobs. The matter was never broached between us. We were variety artists; we were pros. To consider anything else would have been heresy.

6

An experience shared by most of the best-known British comedians who emerged in the immediate post-war period was a date at the Windmill Theatre in London and contact with the man forever associated with this curious theatrical institution—Vivian Van Damm.

Morecambe and Wise are among them, although they would never allow Van Damm to put their names on the list he displayed of the famous who had once trod his boards. I appreciate their point of view. 'He fired us,' Ernie explained. Yes, but Van Damm was also responsible, though indirectly, for starting them on their career in variety. After the Windmill they never looked back.

I knew old VD, as he was affectionately called by his 118 permanent employees at the Windmill. I was at a party there on the night of 4 February, 1948 when VD's little theatre celebrated its sixteenth anniversary of continuous revue, having completed 22,744 performances in 210 editions of a conveyor belt of nudity and entertainment known as Revuedeville. I remember VD's taking me into the wings to give me as a writer a behind-the-scenes view of his star fan dancer, Anita D'Ray, wearing only a pair of black ostrich fans which she waved between herself and a riveted audience straining like leashed pointers in the forward rows of the stalls. For them it was a delightfully provocative dance in which first one pink nipple then another then her beautiful bottom would peep out from between the velvety black feathers.

To see the dance from the wings was like receiving a kick in the solar plexus. Morecambe and Wise saw Anita's dance from the wings. As Ernie recalled, 'If Eric hadn't blinked he would have gone blind.'

VD was a connoisseur; at fifty-nine his palate had matured. He was of the stuff that theatre ghosts are made, for he was not just present at the Windmill, he was a presence there, padding softly along the stone passages with a slight stoop and a sardonic, enquiring smile. He would never enter a dressing room without calling, 'Are you presentable, girls?' though his study of each showgirl's potential as a nude had been careful to say the least. He preferred them to start at fourteen and a half. For the Windmill, figures had to be trim, youthful and well-developed without need of support because, as he told me, 'there isn't a bra in the house.'

He had no time for false modesty. When one girl objected to appearing in gauze, he said, 'But darling, you're quite at liberty to go where it's warmer.'

Born in London, the son of a solicitor, he had been wild and intractable. He had a shrewd head on his shoulders, however. At twenty he bought the rights of a noiseless carburettor from its inventors, two brothers named Holloway, for half-a-crown then sold the Belgian rights for £2,000.

He had drifted into cinema management, invented bucket seats and he had animated silent films with sound effects. He had lost his money in two original ventures, a news theatre and speedway, then gone to work for a rich widow named Laura Henderson who had bought the Palais de Luxe Cinema in Great Windmill Street and converted it into an intimate theatre she renamed the Windmill.

Initially the Windmill lost money. Then in 1937 VD introduced nudes. Before Laura Henderson died in 1944, aged eighty-two, she had lived to see the Windmill's box office pay over £500,000 in entertainment tax. The payroll was £72,000 a year—in a theatre with only 312 seats.

VD was left 20,000 of the Windmill's 22,000 preference shares and found himself in absolute control. But he changed little, except that where Laura Henderson had kept a watchful eye on the private lives of the show girls, VD confined his discipline more to the theatre which was precisely what he had made it.

Every idea bore the stamp of his approval. Only he made decisions, hired or fired artists, opened office mail or passed payments. He had about fifty regular performers on his payroll. These, even before the Health Service, received free medical and dental treatment. They were groomed in elocution, make-up, table manners, dress sense, and taught singing and dancing.

They started on a minimum of £10 a week. Starlets received £16 and individual acts, such as Anita D'Ray, £23. One of these, Marion Lynde, edited the Windmill Camp News.

The girls worked as two companies in a complicated rota of performance and rehearsal so designed as to give each company two and a half weeks' complete rest every eighteen weeks, in addition to their regular two weeks' summer holiday, all on full pay. Some girls had been there ten years; a girl was retired only when she needed to wear a bra.

Eric and Ernie will never forget their audition at the Windmill. They were shown into VD's musty office with rainbow fish in glass tanks, and, on the wall behind the desk, the text, in Gothic lettering, THERE ARE NO POCKETS IN SHROUDS—*Laura Henderson had left £246,191.*

VD was signing letters, his pen scratching loudly across the pile of paper before him.

ERIC He looked up. 'Well, boys, let's see what you can do.' We looked around. It was the smallest room I've been in outside a loo. You could barely open the door.

'The stage isn't very large either,' he said smiling. 'I had a fellow here called Harry Secombe. He did a sort of shaving act. There was another called Dick Emery. He dressed up as a woman. We get all kinds.'

We had heard of neither. Anyhow we went through our complete ten minutes, cross-gags, the lot, less than a yard from VD's nose—he had no sense of smell, by the way.

'All right,' he said, 'you're on—£25 a week for the two of you. I'll engage you for one week with an option for a further five weeks.'

That was for six shows a day, don't forget. Still we couldn't complain. Here was our big chance—of paying Mrs Duer.

At 2.30 on the Sunday was the big undress rehearsal. The place was filled with mums, dads, friends and relations of the cast plus a representative from the Lord Chamberlain's office to see that the statutory decencies were observed.

There were strict notices everywhere forbidding men on pain of instant dismissal from entering the girls' dressing rooms which were under the stage. The notices were unnecessary. In the wings girls, gorgeous girls, stepped out of dressing gowns and stood starkers, waiting to go on.

One said, 'Dammit, Eric, give me a cigarette. I need a drag before the curtain goes up, otherwise I'll get an uncontrollable urge to scratch my bum in the middle of the scene.'

I couldn't hold the lighter steady. 'Oh you silly billy,' she said with a flutter of big violet eyes, 'after you've been here six weeks you won't turn a hair.'

'It will have all fallen out,' I predicted.

Ernie and I went down quite well with the mums and dads, but in the six shows on the Monday, starting at noon, we died six times. We had to follow a sort of orgy act with bare-chested male dancers in tights, cracking whips, girl dancers falling about under psychedelic lighting and nudes everywhere.

The curtain came down on this erotic feast and we stepped on to the apron of the stage to face, not just a reluctant audience, but an audience with the concentrated hate of a lynch-mob. Not one polite snicker met our collection of banal jokes. Later in the day, when men who had queued from ten or eleven in the morning for front row seats and eventually gave these up after about the fourth continuous performance through sheer exhaustion or bladder pressure, their places were taken by others vaulting from behind. It was known as the Windmill Steeplechase, and this event took place during the seven minutes in which we were trying to register.

Actually it was a question of where you appeared on the bill. Harry Worth and Jimmy Edwards with his 'Hullo, music lovers!' did fairly well, as did Arthur English and Gillie Potter. Our place on the bill could not have been worse, and the audience left us with no illusions. On the Tuesday, it was even worse. On the Wednesday, as we entered the stage door, we were stopped by the stage-door keeper, Ben Fuller.

Ben's voice was well known. It reached every room and corridor of the Windmill labyrinth on the public address system whenever a stage-door Johnny called asking to meet a particular girl while the caller stood outside in Archer Street with its out-of-work musicians waiting to be contacted by orchestra fixers.

71

Ben Fuller was brief with us. 'Excuse me, Mr Van Damm would like a word with you in his office.'

'Hullo,' Ernie remarked to me, 'obviously he wants to take up the option.'

'Get your pen out for that contract,' I advised. 'Have it ready.'

We bounced into VD's office.

'Gentlemen,' he said, 'I thought I'd let you know, I won't be taking up the option.'

'What?'

'I'm sorry. My patrons seem to prefer the other double-act, Hank and Scott.'

We were devastated. 'That's impossible.'

'I'm afraid it's true. They get more applause.'

Hank and Scott were Tony Hancock and his partner, Derek Scott.

'B-but Mr Van Damm, we have our career to think about. We've told several agents we're going to be here six weeks.'

'Well boys, you still have the rest of this week to run. I'm sure you can sell yourselves in that time.' He had a voice gravelled by expensive cigars.

Ernie said, 'Mr Van Damm, would you mind if we put an advert in *The Stage* to the effect that Morecambe and Wise are having to leave the Windmill due to prior commitments?'

He smiled. 'By all means.'

That day we wrote to at least twenty variety agents, and on the last day, on Saturday morning, one of them, Gordon Norval, came to see the show. He was a small man with silver hair who had the booking of two minor show dates, the Grand, Clapham, and the Kilburn Empire. We had hoped for bigger fish, anyhow it was something. We couldn't get him a free ticket but VD let us have a box—they were usually empty—for thirteen shillings.

We called round at Gordon Norval's office at 18, Charing Cross Road, on the Monday.

He said, 'Would you boys be free to open at the Grand, Clapham, next week?'

I have always let Ernie do the talking in a situation like this. Not that he's the boss—he's too small for that. But the act has to have one bastard who can say no, and it might as well be him. He made a show of looking in his diary—all it had in it were careful entries of the five bob I had borrowed from him.

He said, 'As a matter of fact, yes, we do happen to be free next week.'

'Ten quid a week for the two of you, less commission?'

'OK.'

'Incidentally, can you do two acts?'

'Of course.'

'I'll make it £12 for the two spots—ten minutes each?'

'It's a deal.'

Outside the office, I said, 'You know what you've done? All we have is ten minutes, even working slowly. You tell me how we can make that into twenty minutes.'

'We'll have to work something out,' Ernie said.

'It's taken us over ten years to work up ten minutes. One minute a year. Now we have to find another ten minutes by next Monday. We'll never do it. I would have been content with one spot for £10.'

Ernie said, 'The trouble with you is that you know nothing about business.'

'Well, he was giving us a quid a minute for the first ten minutes. Then you accept four bob a minute for the second ten minutes. Good business? Ha!'

'You obviously haven't heard of the law of diminishing returns.'

ERNIE   Actually, it was the best thing that could have happened to us. Our backs were to the wall. We went straight back to our bedroom at Mrs Duer's. We had to produce ten whole minutes out of nothing. There were no such things as scriptwriters in those days, not for the likes of us, anyway.

Eric had a tune on his brain called *The Woody Woodpecker's Song*. There was a little trill at the end of each phrase which he could sing with a funny little voice, so I said, 'Let's do that song but with a little patter in which I play up to your ego by saying you have the bigger part, while all I really leave you with is the little trill.'

After some padding and fooling, we built it up into ten minutes, but we didn't take it seriously. Our real act, the hotchpotch we

73

had stolen from all and sundry, was our big turn. This new one was something we were doing for the extra £2.

Well, we got to the Grand. The show was called *Fig Leaves and Apple Sauce*, which will indicate the big attraction—nudes. We were to go on second in the first half, and second after the interval, the two hardest spots on any bill.

We opened with our real act, thinking it would give us a springboard for the other. We died and went off, followed by a 'Clapham silence' which in variety at that time was the next thing to the death knoll.

Depressed, we waited for the *coup-de-grace* from that small, Monday audience of mainly girls eating sweets and nuts while their boy friends kneaded their thighs. To our flabbergasted surprise, our second spot paralysed them, despite the fact that we had followed a spectacular with nudes. The audience fell about, so much so that the following week, Nat Tennens, who smoked a fat cigar and ran the Kilburn Empire, wanted us for his theatre, for the same money.

Now we reversed the order of our acts. We put the Woody Woodpecker routine first. It was so successful that it gave our regular act a new life. Again, so much so, that the following week we went back to the Grand, Clapham, and the week after that we returned to the Kilburn Empire, at the top of the bill.

Meanwhile our money had gone up to £40 a week. We had never made anything like that before, and Gordon Norval, who had done it all, became our unofficial agent. I remember our celebrating in a pub, something we had never done. As the pints came up we soon weren't just beginning to get somewhere, we had made the big time! What a night, but what a hangover.

Meanwhile Doreen Blyth was on tour in a show run by a man called Reggie Dennis. Doreen and I were going steady by this time. She told Reggie Dennis she knew of a 'couple of guys' (which was how we were billed), who might be useful in his show, and he came to Clapham and saw us.

He said, 'How would you like to tour in my revue, *Front Page Personalities?* I'll pay you £27 10s joint.'

We jumped at the offer. It was a good show, touring the Number Two variety circuit, and in it we began to learn about show business. We learnt how to go on and do a few extra minutes off the top, the very thought of which had previously scared us rigid. We learnt how to compere and introduce acts, to go out and get a laugh on just local gags and chat.

The top of the bill was Maurice Fogel, who did a brilliant mind-reading act. Arthur Helliwell of *The People* tried to expose the act as a hoax. Maurice merely pointed out that he had never claimed it was anything more than entertainment, so the 'exposé' merely served as good publicity. Maurice and I are still in touch.

Reggie Dennis did a xylophone act and his wife Sylvia sang. We had the Two Pirates, a comedy act, whom we had met at Mrs Duer's. The Kovaks, a trampoline act, were also in it. There was a line of girls, and there was a girl who was introduced as an ex-British agent who had spent her war in France sending secret messages directing Allied bombers to their targets. After this build-up she would go out and do a striptease.

We were eleven months in Reggie Dennis' show during which we earned regular money, and were able to buy good clothes which were very important in show business then. We got to the great London show date, the Met, Edgware Road, and we began to get the odd mention in local papers. It was a wonderful, happy time which like all good things eventually came to an end.

ERIC By now our act was fairly polished. We were still in the difficult second spot of the show which followed six pretty girls dancing very well. It meant registering immediately.

So we did it this way. Ernie would run on the stage, singing *Heartbreaker*, while I ran on from the opposite side, wearing a funny hat. I would stop and look at him, then slap him across the face as hard as I possibly could. With practice you could make it sound a lot worse than it felt, though there were occasions when the woof was badly timed, and you'd see Ernie's face go white and his eyes pop like marbles.

You'd hear the audience gasp, and I would open with, 'How dare you have the sort of face I dislike!'

From there on the act was at high speed, never waiting for a reaction from the audience. We had modelled ourselves on Sid and Max Harrison, who are the fathers of Hope and Keen. Only the Americans were doing the lazy stuff in those days, the Americans and Dickie Henderson.

In ten minutes we would pack in about forty gags, sing a couple of songs, and do a tap dance with two or three acrobatic falls.

Gags?

I would run on with a telegram and say, 'Read that. It's a telegram from my wife. She's just given birth to triplets. Three of them.'

Ernie   Triplets!

Eric   What am I going to do? I've no money.

Ernie   You'll have to go out to work.

Eric   Oh, will I?

Ernie   Can you drive a bus?

Eric   No.

Ernie   Can you mow a lawn?

Eric   No.

Ernie   Can you dig a ditch.

Eric   No.

Ernie   What can you do?

Eric   I just handed you a telegram. I can produce triplets.

Ernie   Matter of fact, I didn't know you were married.

Eric   It was one of those quiet weddings.

Ernie   Quiet weddings?

Eric   I didn't go.

Ernie   Where did you meet her?

Eric   Who?

Ernie   Your wife.

Eric   Oh, the wife. At a dance. She was the prettiest thing on the ballroom floor. I can see her now—lying there.

Ernie   What did you do?

Eric   The only thing I could do. I gave her artificial recreation.

Ernie   You mean respiration. Recreation is when you have fun.

Eric   I'm no mug.

Ernie   Did you meet her mother?

Eric   Her mother?—A military policeman with bloomers. What a family. There's her brother—

Ernie   Her brother?

Eric   He lived with me and I told him, 'You can treat my house as if it were your own.'

Ernie And did he?

Eric Yes, he sold it this morning.

Ernie Tell me about the day you became engaged.

Eric Ah, I bought her an engagement ring. You should have seen it. It had five stones. Not diamonds. Just stones. Five big bricks. She walked about all on one side. She has left me now. I've forgotten what she looked like. (In pain) Ah!

Ernie What's the matter?

Eric I just remembered.

Ernie Why don't you tell the police.

Eric I would but they wouldn't believe it.

Ernie Have you any advice for all the young married men in the audience tonight?

Eric As a matter of fact I have. Men, married men, young married men, remember that your wives still enjoy chocolates, sweets, perfume, flowers. Let her see that you haven't forgotten. Mention them occasionally.

In the first spot we always finished on the Woody Woodpecker routine, for which the publishers of the song had done us a special arrangement. The second spot was the same sort of thing but a little more relaxed.

ERNIE We owe a lot at this stage not only to Reggie Dennis, but to the Two Pirates, Jock Cochrane and Reggie Mankin; the former died a few years ago. When the show was coming to an end in the autumn of 1950, they mentioned us to an agent named Frank Pope who booked for two top variety circuits, Butterworth's and the Moss Empires.

Frank Pope came up to Grimsby to see the show and he agreed to take us on. We had no contract with Gordon Norval; anyhow, the two agents came to an amicable and satisfactory arrangement between themselves and we signed what is called a sole agency agreement with Frank Pope which meant that he guaranteed us a minimum of £10 a week and we had to give him six months' notice by registered post if we wanted to opt out.

The first date he got us was with Joseph Locke topping the bill. It was at the Empire, Swansea, where Eric and I had first met in 1939. In eleven years we had climbed to £35 a week.

77

PART TWO

Main Dish

7

ERNIE The Moss Empire circuit of theatres was in the First
Division of British variety. There were about twenty Empires
in the early fifties, all well-run theatres, with the Finsbury Park
Empire, in London, as their show date and a stepping stone to the
most prestigious variety date in Britain, or for that matter the
world, the London Palladium, near Oxford Circus. To top the bill
at the Palladium was the apex of our ambition. Our sights were set
on this peak.

The booker for the circuit was a very shrewd woman called
Cissy Williams. She would go on a Monday to the first house at
Finsbury Park, and you watched your step. You might get a
message from her to change this or that in your act, and you did as
she said, no question about it. I remember she would never allow
us to have a blackout and spotlight for a song. She paid £35 a week
for the second spot with an extra £10 a week if you went to the
Glasgow Empire, partly because of the rail fare but mainly because the place was a house of terror. It was known in the profession as the Graveyard of English comics.

It was a beautifully run theatre, with a fine canteen, lifts, marble
staircases, everything always excessively clean, even to the chande-
liers that sparkled and the golden cherubs near the ceiling on whom
there was never so much as a speck of dust. The doorman was a
magnificent giant.

ERIC He could have put Ernie in his pocket and still had room for his pipe.

ERNIE But you felt you were a foreigner. Nobody spoke to you and the audiences were hard—hard to please, hard to satisfy. I cannot think of a greater ordeal for an English comic than a nine-minute second spot on the bill in a first house at the Glasgow Empire.

I can remember our first time there, coming off to the sound of our own footsteps, and the fireman on duty in the wings saying, 'Och, they're beginning to like you!'

Eric has a gag he sometimes does at show business parties. It goes like this, 'Folks, I'll now do an impression of my friend Des O'Connor doing his opening second spot at the Glasgow Empire: "Ladies and gentlemen . . . thud!" '

ERIC Yes, that's right, and I'll tell you the story behind it. Poor old Des, it was the time when Des really stood for desperate, one of the big traumas in his trauma-studded life. The first act on that bill at the Glasgow Empire was a very popular Glaswegian husband and wife team, Dorothy Reid and MacKenzie, who sang and played the accordian. Just a week before Des' debut in Glasgow, the husband was knocked down by a tram and killed. The tragedy was reported with big headlines in the local papers. Dorothy, in the spirit of the real trouper, insisted on going ahead with her act with her nephew. It took real guts on her part to go on the stage and sing songs like *Will Ye No' Come Back Again?* To see her fighting back the tears was enough to choke up any audience. Unfortunately for Des, he had to go on next with the funnies. Day after day he died, and it wasn't just apathy from the audience. It was a sullen resentment that seemed to convey to him that he should be dead, not poor MacKenzie.

Des was unnerved. He got worse and worse. He couldn't eat. He vomited in the wings. One afternoon he went to the cinema and came out without knowing what the film was about. Finally, on the Thursday, he was in his attic dressing-room when he heard people yelling for him. Dorothy Reid had suddenly become very upset on the stage and had cut short her act.

Des came pounding down the iron staircase and rushed on the stage to be met by a terrible silence from a packed house of 3,000 choked up because of Dorothy and staring up at him with pure hate. Des panicked. He told the same story twice, then the end of one before the beginning. It didn't matter because nobody would have laughed anyway. The thought of going on became too much. The only possible escape he could see was by throwing a phoney faint, which he did, and he was carried off the stage. *Thud*.

We played the Glasgow Empire with Lena Horne and later Issy Bonn at the top of the bill. We found that if the tops were liked, as these were, the rest of the bill were tolerated, even appreciated, depending of course on the day of the week. Monday was always terrible.

ERNIE The managers of those Moss Empires were men of authority; you treated them with respect. They formally met and greeted each performer at bandcall which by tradition was at eleven on the Monday morning. I remember our first time at Glasgow, the manager saying, 'Don't worry. This may be the Glasgow Empire but there's no need to be frightened of it. Everybody gets the bird on Friday night and, remember, no football gags on Saturday night. You know?—Celtic and Rangers. Either way, *you* can't win.'

Though the Empires were all well-run theatres, each had its own atmosphere. We always liked working the Swansea Empire —it was a happy place. The Sheffield Empire was cosy. The Liverpool Empire was comfortable—it had a bathroom with a shower to every dressing room, as had the Palace, Manchester, another theatre of the Moss circuit. The Palace had an opulent air. The Empire orchestras were all excellent, and back-stage you'd find everything spotless and well-organised which meant the stage-managers were good. Back-stage was the stage-manager's domain, and nobody used the pass door to the auditorium without his permission.

Another important personage in a theatre was the stage-door keeper, and again those employed by the Moss Empire circuit were the cream of their profession. The stage-door keeper often took care of artists' laundry. It went out on a Monday and came back on the Friday, and woe betide you if you didn't pay your bill. I remember asking one stage-door keeper who they had had at the top of the bill the previous week. He mentioned a very famous personality, adding, 'But we won't have him here again. He owes me three and six for his laundry.'

You will hear old pros tell you that the twenties were the heyday of music hall, or variety, as it became known, and that by 1939 it was already dying, that the cinema was killing it. Yet, when we started in 1939, variety was still doing good business; indeed it was booming. We believe that if anything killed variety it was the war when a lot of brilliant acts disappeared and the Palladium embarked on a policy of using only American tops of the bill of the Las Vegas level. This did nothing to help British artists, and on top of that TV was on the ascendency despite the pundits who scoffed at the new medium. 'TV will never kill variety,' we heard so many say. 'Who'll bother to watch a small screen when you can see acts live in the theatre?'

To get back to bandcalls, a certain protocol had to be observed. Your bandbooks were picked up in the order in which they were put down on the apron of the stage from right to left. In other words, first come first served, and it was important if you were in a hurry. The star of the show might occupy the band for an hour or more.

I remember one MD (musical director) who was terribly particular about the condition of bandparts as they were presented to him.

'This music is very tatty,' he would say.

The artist would then be expected to reply, 'Well, would you mind rewriting it for me?'

This the MD would do, and of course charge a handsome fee for the service. It was politic at that theatre to take the hint.

There were some wonderful characters in variety in those days —people like Mr Caplin, the MD at Finsbury Park Empire, always immaculate in his tail suit and spotless white gloves; or Mr Matthews, the manager at the Metropolitan, Edgware Road, a bulbous man, again in immaculate tails. You felt honoured if one of these superb personages so much as spoke to you.

It you asked me how the time-honoured habit of tipping got to restaurants, I would say from the theatres. For those of us who trod the boards tips supplied the oil that lubricated the machinery of variety.

Eric and I used to have a standing gag. As we came into a theatre we would say, 'Boys, what's it to be this week, crinkle (paper money) or chink (coins)?'

'Do you mean that or is it a line from your act?'

'Try us.'

The customary rate varied with your place on the bill and the tipee. For us in those days it was: to the stage-door keeper—five bob (chink); to the fellow who went around on a Saturday night picking up bandbooks from the orchestra and returning them to artists, an important man to remember if you were on the second spot in the second house and didn't want to wait until the end of the show for your bandbooks—a half-crown (chink); to the electrician—seven and six (chink); to the stage-manager—thirty bob (crinkle and chink). The MDs were above it until the top American acts started coming over. These super-stars with their super-salaries were tip drunk. They even tipped the audience.

At the end of a summer season, the top of the bill would normally be expected to part with between £50 and £100 in crinkle, though we do know a few household names who didn't!

ERIC The life we led on a variety tour? On a typical day you rose at about ten, had breakfast and sauntered down to the theatre to see if there was any mail for you. God, it was tough. You might look at a copy of *The Performer* or *The Stage* and put it back on the rack. The acrobats, jugglers, trapeze acts, balancing acts and other specialities, would be there, on the stage, rehearsing, some having been at it since nine. The children would be going through their paces, their parents watching them. The only people who didn't rehearse were the comics.

Girls in the dance acts also worked hard. Besides having to practice a lot, they often travelled with steps and platforms and other props which they had to pack and manhandle themselves together with their skips full of their sequinned dresses and frilly knickers. They had to keep these clean and ironed, and on Mondays they always wanted to wash their hair.

Ernie and I would be interested in the girls in a show; we'd probably try to date a couple—for a coffee at the nearest Kardomah or Lyons. We'd get back to the theatre by a quarter to one, more or less to check that everything was all right before it closed at one.

On a Tuesday, you would buy the local paper to see if you'd been written up in it, though you'd never admit to bothering to read it. You'd go back to your digs for lunch. You'd have had your card signed by the theatre manager which got you into the cinemas free, so you'd go to a film in the afternoon, leaving about 4.30 to have your tea at the digs and get to the theatre by 5.30. As Harry Worth used to say, 'Show business is OK if it wasn't for that bit of unpleasantness between 6.15 and 10.45.'

After the shows, the older pros generally went to a pub. We'd return to our digs for supper, and after that we'd do nothing but talk show business till two or three in the morning when at last we went to bed. As far as I was concerned, it was a pleasant and easy life—Ernie has made that point. Besides, the prospects seemed bright. We knew comics, steady old troupers, earning £60 to £100 a week as second tops of the bill, who had been doing a total of maybe twenty minutes a show for fifty-two weeks a year, using material not a word of which had been changed in the past two or three decades. And, before the variety theatres began to close in the early fifties, date books could be filled without any difficulty, if you were well-known, for four or five years in advance.

As for material, comics just lifted most of it from others before them. An original joke was a rare treat, so much so that when the American comics started coming over to this country with their ultra-smart, electric-blue suits and their intense professionalism in that they worked very hard and paid well for fresh material, many British comics were finished practically overnight.

Ernie and I might well have been casualties too only for an incident that happened during a summer season when we appeared at the Winter Garden Theatre in Blackpool. Topping the bill was Alan Jones, the American singer (*The Donkey Serenade*), father of the pop singer, Jack Jones. From time to time Alan would lose his voice—the Blackpool air is notorious for the effect it has on singers' throats. Whenever this happened, Eve Boswell would come across from another theatre, the Opera House, and double for him. George and Alfred Black were presenting our show. They said, 'Boys, in case anything happens to Alan and he can't perform, we want you two to stand by to go on and fill in for him until Eve arrives.'

Now, we had no idea of how we could possibly fill in for Alan Jones. We had two double-act routines that we would have used up by the time he came on at the end. We had nothing left over and we possessed no concert party warm-up gifts. One day we were in our dressing room when we heard Alan start his song. After a few notes the song stopped abruptly and we heard him say, 'I'm sorry, ladies and gentlemen, but I'm afraid I can't continue. My voice has been affected by the sea air.' Immediately Ernie and I took off all our clothes in our dressing-room. Alfred Black came running in and said, 'Quick boys, on the stage.' But we said, 'No we can't, we've no clothes on.'

Black was furious. He had to go on the stage himself and explain to the audience that the emergency had been taken care of, and that Eve Boswell was being rushed over to entertain them.

That night Ernie and I said very little. We were both shaken to the core. We had let the Blacks down for the simple reason that we had no material in reserve, besides being incapable of going on and just chatting to an audience in a relaxed way about funny things we had seen happening all around us in Blackpool.

'We'll never get anywhere like this,' I said.

'I agree,' Ernie said.

'It's a ridiculous plight for two so-called comics.'

'Absurd.'

But instead of working out something together, as we had done when Gordon Norval wanted an extra ten minutes for £2, we started looking for material we could crib. It was Bobby Dennis who gave us our next routine when we met him on a train.

He said, 'Boys, I've got something I'm sure you could do very well.'

It went like this:

Ernie You should get away from it all. You should go somewhere exciting—Spain.

Eric Spain?

Ernie Majorca, the Costa Brava.

Eric How much?

Ernie You would make a marvellous bullfighter.

Eric   You're only saying that.

Ernie   No, I'm not.

Eric   Well, somebody just did.

Ernie   We'll have to dress you for the part. You must look right.

Eric   A right what?

Ernie   A right bullfighter. Now, you're wearing a three-cornered hat.

Eric   What for?

Ernie   Your three-cornered head.

Eric   You're getting them in, aren't you?

Ernie   You're wearing a blue velvet jacket with a ruffle collar, a spangled shirt with lace cuffs, bright yellow pantaloons, snuggly fitting of course, white stockings, and a most heavenly pair of black patent shoes. What do you say to that?

Eric   I won't have to say anything. Dressed like that I would think everybody would know.

Ernie   Now, what are you going to call yourself?

Eric   How about Elsie?

Ernie   Choose a strong name—a bullfighting name.

Eric   How about Arterio Cordova Liquorice?

Ernie   That's not a bullfighting name.

Eric   But it's Spanish, isn't it? (*Liquorice in the North is called Spanish*).

Ernie   How about Morecambe from England?

Eric   How about Trembling from Fear?

Ernie   Now comes the great day. You are standing in the centre of the bullring, eyes everywhere focused on you. They are all waiting for you to do something. Suddenly there's a cloud of dust as the bull rushes in.

Eric   And there's a bigger cloud of dust as I rush out.

Ernie   You're not a coward, are you?

Eric   Yes.

Ernie   What a magnificent animal that is. It's sitting behind that post.

Eric   It's a sitting bull.

Ernie   He's fast asleep.

Eric   He's a bulldozer.

Ernie Now comes your supreme moment. The moment of the kill. Just you and the bull alone. Suddenly you whip out your *machotte*. (*Bobby's word derived probably from machete.*)

Eric Pardon?

Ernie I said, you suddenly whip out your *machotte*.

Eric How big is my *machotte*?

Ernie Your *machotte* is over two feet long.

Eric That's a lot of *machotte*.

Ernie Suddenly the bull rushes towards you and you stick your *machotte* between the bull's eyes. You kill it with one master stroke.

Eric I'm really quite a *machotte* stroker. What's that up in the box?

Ernie The President of the bullring.

Eric Does he know?

Ernie He has awarded you the ear of the bull. This is a great honour. You must thank him in the old Spanish way.

Eric What way is that?

Ernie Same as the English, only quicker.

Eric Muchos gracias, Senor—quanta lagusta Edmundo Ros.

Ernie Viva Zapata.

(*Together*) With chips.

Ernie Now you walk towards the President's box. You throw the ear of the bull to the President's beautiful daughter.

Eric I'm glad, I wouldn't have known what to do with it.

Ernie She looks down at you and smiles. She says—

Eric I know what she says.

Ernie What does she say?

Eric Hullo, hullo, hullo—what's this 'ear?

(*And finishing together, singing*) I'll raise a bunion on his Spanish onion if I catch him bending tonight! Olez!

ERNIE The original routine Bobby Dennis gave us was a lot more suggestive. We cleaned it up a bit and wowed the audience with it in the opening spot at the Central Pier, Blackpool. Peter Webster, who owned the theatre, came running backstage, saying he had never known anyone to get laughs like that so early in the show. Even so, Eric and I found the routine still a bit too strong. We kept toning it down until we eventually got to the stage where we didn't even bring in the *machotte*. There is a point after which blue material ceases to be funny. This varies with every comedian or act, but we have always had to be extremely careful otherwise we would provoke a flood of complaining letters. On TV we have to be even more careful. Audience letters are our guide—it takes as few as four to persuade us to modify a line or an innuendo.

ERIC The vital ingredient of good comedy is originality. Most comedians start out as impressionists, but if they don't develop past that stage they never become big names. I wonder how many fellows doing second spots on comedy bills wept when Al Jolson died. There was a lull, I remember. Then you heard them bringing him back—'Ladies and gentlemen, I will now do an impression of the late and great Al Jolson.' I must have seen at least forty versions of the Hollywood Party—'Ah, and who's that coming round the corner but Jimmy Durante—"Ha cha cha . . ." '

Of course, there were and are some brilliant exponents of the impressionist's art. What I am trying to say is that for a performer to progress beyond it he needs to develop his own style and material. But we weren't developing either, for the whole of our basic act was a collection of pirated gags. We went on lifting other people's material, like the beard routine we took from Abbott and Costello.

ERNIE It was a good one, though. I would tell Eric to get off the stage—a lot of double-act cross-talk is based on the 'Get off, I never want to see you again!' opener. I would start singing a song when Eric would reappear, walking backwards but wearing a beard with a cigar attached so that when he took the cigar out of his mouth the beard came away too. I would grab him by the back.

'How dare you come back.' But on swinging him round and seeing the beard I would apologise, 'Oh, I beg your pardon. I *am* terribly sorry.'

On which Eric would look at the audience, remove the cigar and the beard, and say, 'Oh, that's all right.' Then he'd put it back, and to me, 'Not at all.'

'I know a fellow exactly like you.'

'Tall, slim, distinguished-looking, wearing glasses?'

'Except that you have a beard,' I would reply. 'If you see him, let me know.'

Eric, removing the cigar and beard: 'Certainly.'

'Thank you.'

After which he'd put back the beard upside down and run off the stage, to return with another prop.

Occasionally on TV, when Johnny Ammonds, our producer, wants a prop gag, we dig up one of these out of the past.

ERIC There was a charming little dance gag we borrowed from 'Monsewer' Eddie Gray who used to wear a top hat and old-style beard, and at one time worked with the Crazy Gang. I would go off the stage and come back with a sheet of music under my arm.

'What's that?' Ernie would ask.

'My dance routine.'

'Your dance routine?'

'Yes.'

'Why isn't it with the Musical Director?'

'Because I've got to dance to it.' On which I would put it on the floor, do a tap dance, pretending to read it, then pick it up and walk off.

ERNIE Those variety bills of twenty years ago followed the music hall pattern except that the order of a bill had become more or less set. Usually a variety show began with a dance act, two girls or perhaps two girls and a boy who did about ten minutes, finishing on a very fast routine. They earned about £25 a week.

The second spot followed that. It was where every comic served his apprenticeship and out of which he dreamed he would rise to an easier, better paid and more prestigious position on the bill. I have told you what we received as second spots.

Next came a speciality act on roller skates, or the slack wire, or it might be jugglers, or a dog act, or a balancing act, or a team of acrobats. The speciality act took ten minutes and earned about £45, after which the second top of the bill came on and closed the first half. He was usually a comic and earned, as we did ourselves before long, about £100 a week.

The second half of the show again opened with dancers, the same ones as before if the management was trying to cut back on the bill. Again they were followed by the second second spot comic, then perhaps by some sort of musical act, which earned about £50 and after that for a good half hour the top of the bill on about £300. And in those days we worked with people like Lena Horne, Joan Regan, Eve Boswell, the Nicholas Brothers, the Merry Macs, Dickie Henderson, Randolph Sutton, Ruby Murray, Alma Cogan, David Hughes, David Whitfield, Yana, Ray Ellington and his Orchestra, Joe Loss and his Orchestra, Anne Shelton, and even Phyllis Dixie.

Once we took out a bill of our own costing £250 in salaries to the other artists on it. By the Friday we'd probably have taken £200. Then on the Saturday we'd take about £500. We'd be on a fifty-fifty basis with the management which meant that we averaged about £100 a week. You felt good being in a position to pay out the pros, but it was a lot more profitable to us at the time to go on a bill and earn a salary.

ERIC I may be mistaken, but you no longer see speciality acts of the quality you had on variety bills in those days. Cycling acts like the Wonder Wheelers—we used to go about with one of the daughters; or balancing acts like Jacky, the Dutch boy, who would balance on his hands on wooden blocks on a pedestal, building up his pile of bricks until he was practically out of sight; tableau acts with men and girls in white riding white horses with white dogs; knife- and axe-throwing acts; trampoline and tightrope acts; speciality dance acts with acrobatic dancers, rag doll dancers, Egyptian hieroglyphic dancers, sand dancers and mechanical dancers; wonderful speciality sketches like Old Mother Riley and Kitty; illusionists like Lionel King, who would get three people on the stage, then go into the audience and play them in a game of poker from the auditorium, and win every time.

Once he was picked up by three card-sharpers on a train who took him for a sucker. Lionel cleaned them out.

There was Eddie Gordon and Nancy. Eddie was a real American burlesque type who went on the stage dressed as a clown and worked with a very pretty girl. He was always first in the theatre, hours before anybody else. You'd see a figure emerge from a dark corner and it would be Eddie in full make-up and costume. There was old Tattersall who did a speciality vent act with life-

Morecambe, Talent Contest Champ, 1938

Alice and Rosie Lloyd who helped plan our debut

Two travelling mums, Sadie and Mrs Tolcher, with Morecambe
(before Wise) and discovery, Helvig Rintala

Jean Bamforth (*top*) and Mary
Naylor with Stan Vassey scoring
a try

Discoveries in Plymouth during
Dunkirk week. Dorothy Duval
(*left*), Tommy Thompson, Mary
Naylor and Millicent Phillips

Harry Bristoe whose voice
broke before his braces

Arthur Tolcher with mouth
organ sandwich

A certain smile

and a poorly look—in 1941

Strike a New Note was the smash hit of 1942. Sid Field became a-
star overnight and we learnt all about the birds and the bees
Below: Sid Field and his leading lady, Zoë Gail

Guest stars with *Youth Takes a Bow*—Billy Cotton (*Oh What a Lovely Bunch of Coconuts*) Tommy Handley (The Disorderly Room) Dave Morris and Jack Warner ('Mind my bike')

On the air for the first time as a double-act in *Beginners Please*

In Circus and Variety we learnt the facts of life—we took a cut,
and Ernie's voice immediately broke

size dummies that he built himself. Worked by clockwork, they breathed, they walked about. I wouldn't be surprised if they even had a bit on the side, though they were usually Chelsea pensioners and their ninety-year-old molls.

There was a wonderful story about the time Tattersall was playing the Theatre Royal, Hanley. On the Saturday night after the last show, he came out of the theatre, packed his dummies into his station wagon and was about to leave when he saw Lynda and Lana, two dancers, standing forlornly in the rain waiting for a taxi.

'Would you like a lift?' he enquired gallantly.

'Oh, thank you,' the girls said.

'You're a bit crowded,' said Lynda.

'Not at all, my dear. All we need do is stow my gear a little more sensibly.'

With that he took his dummy old lady out of the station wagon, propped her up against the wall near the stage-door, loaded the girls' props and luggage into the vehicle, got in with the girls, and drove off to Newcastle, leaving the old lady by the stage-door.

Meanwhile she had been found by the Leeds police. They spoke to her but she refused to answer. The Leeds Royal Infirmary medical staff were consulted, an ambulance team arrived, they tried to wake her.

'She's breathing, so she must be alive,' said the doctor.

He shook her. She did not respond.

'We can of course arrest her,' said a young constable.

'On what charge?' his superior demanded.

'What about loitering with intent?'

'You bloody fool—and make ourselves the laughing stock of the Constabulary? Does the old dear look as though she could do *anything*, much less commit a felony?'

'Causing an obstruction?' suggested another constable.

'The owner of the property will have to make a complaint. And he won't because he would be made to look an ogre in the local papers.'

'Leave her alone,' said a passer-by. 'She's doing nobody any harm.'

'But it's raining. She must be cold and hungry. We can't leave her here. She looks like my mother, God bless her soul.'

So it went on until a telegram arrived from Newcastle, and the police, very red-faced, took over the dummy and lodged it in the left-luggage office at Leeds Central Station.

ERNIE   It was the age of the Lord Chamberlain's censors. There were officials who dived into scripts like demented dentists extracting the wrong teeth. Sketches and revues had to be censored but comedy acts were left to the discretion of the comic, and of course, the managements. Max Miller would bait an audience. He would come on with his two 'joke' books. 'Which one do you want—the Red Book or the Blue Book?' he'd ask. Back would come the roar, 'THE BLUE BOOK!'

Remember it was the age of variety, 'refined' music hall, full of false modesty and out-moded prudery at a time when the word 'bloody' *on the stage* shocked people. Or, rather, shocked officialdom. They could descend on a theatre manager's head like a swarm of bees. All he could do, poor man, to protect himself, was bring down the curtain when a comedian overstepped the mark. Max Miller's curtain droppers are legendary and legends grow. The first, I believe, followed a throw-away line when he said that something was 'like the little girl who swallowed a pin and didn't feel the prick till she was sixteen.'

The second? I have heard it was more involved. About a stunt man who was doing a tightrope act over a gorge with a raging river in the canyon below. To his consternation who should he meet on the rope coming in the opposite direction but a stunt girl.

'What should he do?' Max asked his audience. 'Go back or toss himself off?' Curtain.

Max, with his bright check suits and plus-fours, was among the last of the comics to wear comedy outfits. They had gone out by the time we came on the scene. The American stand-up comics had shown us how to be funny, standing in front of a curtain and rattling off a string of chatty gags based more or less on domestic situations. We naturally emulated them, but whereas previously we had sounded pure American, we now reverted to our normal accents.

94

We worked steadily through 1951 and were booked more or less solid for the whole of 1952. We had done two pantomimes, at Brighton and at Swansea, and a summer season at Blackpool, and we were booked for a third pantomime at the Theatre Royal, Sheffield. I suppose by midsummer 1952 you could say we were beginning to climb in the variety league.

ERIC On HMS *Victory* there is a little plaque which marks the spot where Nelson fell. In the Empire, Edinburgh, there should have been a plaque to mark the spot where Eric Morecambe fell. Like Nelson I had met my Waterloo or am I making a mess of history? My marks at school were always very low but you know what I mean. Before me unrolls a carpet and I take the first step on it. Ernie's eyes pop like marbles, his face white, as though I had fetched him a shock open-hander.

8

A double-act is not an easy relationship to share, and for those on the outside it is even less easy to understand. Its nuances would certainly be worth exploring if you could get say six pairs together in a psychiatrist's consulting room, inject them with a truth drug, and let them talk. What a documentary that would make.

In show business a double-act is thought of as a kind of stage marriage—one that's consummated before an audience with the partners super-charged with adrenalin in mixed states of euphoria, anxiety, fear, excitement. Every performer is transformed on the stage; he becomes a projection of himself into an image of his choosing. In a comedy double-act there are two such projections sparking off each other. A suppressed rivalry exists on and off the stage. They vie for acclaim, each believing he is really the star of the team. Few double-acts survive the stresses to which they are subjected. One pair I could mention were known to argue constantly in their dressing-room, each shushing the other to keep his voice down. Even shushing the other whenever they resorted to fisticuffs.

You'd hear, 'Take that, you bastard—(biff)— shush!' Then biff, biff, biff. 'Shush!'

After a while they would emerge with fixed smiles to stand in the wings ready to go on the stage.

Morecambe and Wise do not row but they do disagree, but this they feel is necessary to the way they think and work together. As professionals both are highly sensitive, self-critical and objective. Both readily accept they are necessary to each other yet are glad to be so, for each is the other's greatest fan, they swear. Such a rapport is extremely rare in the profession.

Obviously it is a big factor in their outstanding success, and for it they certainly have to thank Sadie Bartholomew who brought them together and made them think of each other as brothers.

'Ernie was every bit as much to me as my own son,' she told me. 'I treated them alike. If I knitted a pair of socks for one, I knitted a pair for the other. During the war, when things were short, if I got hold of something like an orange I kept it until I had two so that they could have one each—together.'

During their lean period in London the boys had been inseparable, and once they got regular work and began to develop their act their bond deepened. They toured at first in Woody, an ex-WD van with a hood at the back, that they bought for £190 from a builder in Llanelly of all places and sold after a few months because it kept breaking down. Then Ernie heard of a 36-seater bus that had been converted into a caravan, and they bought it for £350 in the hope that they would save on rent and rail fares.

It would help at this stage to introduce a bit of sex, but the truth is that there just hadn't been any. We have noted some voyeurism from the little window at the Prince of Wales Theatre involving the entire cast of Strike a New Note—*except* Ernie.

'Eric was not far wrong when he called him Lilywhite,' Sadie said. 'Because Ernie—and it's the absolute truth—has a genuine purity of heart. He wouldn't look through that window because he couldn't bear the thought of invading other people's privacy. Nobody has ever heard Ernie swear.'

The boys had separately and together taken out the odd girl, but, in Eric's words, 'When we had the time to chase girls we didn't have the money, and when we had the money we were working so hard we never had the time.'

Besides, Ernie was 'going steady' with Doreen. He saw her on occasional week-ends when they were near enough to her home in Peterborough to risk the trip in Woody.

In the spring of 1952, when the courtship had lasted seven years, Sadie tackled Ernie about it.

She said, 'Ernie, when are you getting married?'

'Oh, sometime, I expect. Look, don't you start about me getting married because I'm not getting married until Eric gets married.'

'Why?'

'Well, for one reason, who's going to keep him out of trouble. For another, I'm not going to give a woman my pay packet and have him standing there laughing at me.'

That was how matters stood when they got to Edinburgh in June 1952. They were second comics on the bill being topped by Gipsy Rose Lee at the Empire.

ERIC   I remember it was at bandcall on a Monday morning. We used to look forward to bandcall to study form—there were always pretty girls in the chorus. It was fun making smart-alec approaches. Then I saw this tall girl, very beautiful with wonderful eyes and a sort of sweetness that makes your knees buckle, and I knew immediately she was the one for me for life. Yes, it was as sudden as that. There was never any doubt about it. Somebody introduced us and I learnt her name was Joan Bartlett. I asked her out for a coffee after bandcall, and promptly set about working out a devious plan for campaign with only one thing in mind.

JOAN   Actually it was the most unromantic thing in the world because I was as miserable as sin. I was filling in for another girl in the show and didn't like the job at all. I was interested only in singing. I had been appearing as a soubrette, an interesting part in which you sang a little, danced a little and did odd lines for the comics. Then Lew and Leslie Grade were keen to promote me as a solo artist—this was before the days of Joan Regan and Alma Cogan, and I spent six months rehearsing an act for which the clothes cost £180, a fortune to me. But the Grades hadn't been able to get me the sort of break I had been waiting for. Then a call had come from them. There was a job going at the Edinburgh Empire where a girl in the show had been rushed to hospital for an emergency operation. Could I take her place? I had the right height and figure and it would mean a little extra money until something better came along. Broke, I agreed. It was just a walk-on part and very dull, and it really depressed me for some reason, probably because I was beginning to realise that my chances of making it as a singer were receding, and I was having to face up to this fact, unpleasant as it was.

The day I met Eric must have been awful for him. I had a boy friend at the time whose birthday was coming up. So after the coffee Eric and I went round the shops looking for something to buy the boy friend. In the end we settled for a silver tankard. Eric has had a 'thing' about tankards ever since!

After that it was fate because I found myself on the same bill as Eric and Ernie in three different places. Then they went to Margate. I had said, 'If you can't find digs, try my mother's place —she and my brother run a hotel.' Which the boys did. As it happened, that same week I was playing in Morecambe and I managed to get fixed up at Eric's parent's place, and they told me all the secrets of their son's life!

After that we started to see each other regularly. At week-ends Eric would take a train after his show had ended on a Saturday night to wherever I was playing, and we'd spend the Sunday out somewhere. Some week-ends I would do the travelling. It was a courtship of snatched moments. Then Eric and Ernie, who had been booked for every week of the year, managed to get one week off. The following week they were to do a Radio Luxembourg broadcast with Tessie O'Shea from the Palladium on the Monday and then go on to Sheffield to open in pantomime. It looked like a chance to get married and, very much on the spur of the moment and not very sensibly we decided to take it, hoping the haste would not appear too indecent!

It proved a madly hectic week during which Eric went up to his parents' home at Morecambe; he was then to come down to London where we would meet. We both had wedding outfits to buy, besides a whole lot of other shopping. I had managed to persuade the vicar of St John's Church in Margate to marry us on the Sunday; normally vicars prefer not to have weddings on the Sabbath but I explained our difficulties. Usually it's the only free day in the week a pro has if he is lucky enough to be working. Then of all things fog clamped down on England, so you can imagine the state of Eric's nerves—he has a horror of being late for anything—until the Saturday when the fog lifted. He was waiting at the church when I arrived a little after 3 pm on 11 December 1952. Fortunately my family were in the catering trade, so the reception was no problem.

We spent the wedding night at the Cumberland Hotel in

London, most of the time actually going over the script for the radio broadcast.

Ernie was best man. Cautious by nature, he had found it hard to believe that Eric had become serious about Joan in such a short time. The speed with which events and emotions overtook Ernie left him shaken and dazed, rather like Bernie Winters was when Mike and his wife Cassie decided to get married. Bernie, the remaining bachelor and the younger and larger brother, insisted on coming on the honeymoon. As children they had played together with their cigarette cards. On tour together in their double-act they had played Scrabble, and the thought that their games might end proved too much for Bernie. On the first night of the honeymoon, he kept the groom engaged in game after game of Scrabble while Cassie sat waiting for bed. At two in the morning Mike finally got up.

'Just one more game,' Bernie begged.

ERNIE No, I didn't go on Eric's honeymoon. I was only too happy to leave him safely in his bride's capable hands. I felt like a mother with an unmarriageable daughter that's miraculously swept off her hands by an unsuspecting suitor. I showered my blessings on their holy alliance though it worried my conscience that I hadn't warned Joan about what she was letting herself in for. No, it was a good thing I hadn't—the shock might have been too much. Let her find out gently for herself. Let love discover a way to help her cope, because Eric is no ordinary mortal. His mother had a word for him—Jifflearse, which I must say seemed perfectly to fit. Normally you couldn't move him unless it was for one of his three favourite pastimes—painting (he can't paint); fishing (he's never caught anything); and going to the cinema (it doesn't matter what he sees as long as the picture moves).

When we were out of work, he must have seen every film that came to the local cinema—while I was out doing the business and seeing agents!

It was the same when we were in digs on tour. He would hardly stop, even to have his meal. His soup would appear before him and disappear like lightning. Then he'd say to the landlady, 'Ah, hm, what's next?'

She'd tell him.

'Oh, all right, could I have mine now?—I'm in a bit of a hurry.'

She would oblige. Then he'd be asking for his pudding before anybody else had finished soup.

ERIC That's true. Many were the times I'd be on my pudding before the echo of Ernie's soup had died away.

ERNIE One thing I'll say for Eric, he avoided trouble. I remember one time we were in digs at Brighton. Besides ourselves at the table, there were Billy Dainty and his wife Sandra. Eric as usual was in a hurry.

The food was terrible. I think I am easy-going but I have a point of no return. None of us could touch the food, so when the woman came back into the room I said, 'Excuse me, could I have a word with you?' Silence all round the table.

'Yes?' said the woman.

'I'm sorry, but I'm afraid we can't stay here.'

'Oh?'

'I'm afraid that this is not up to the standard we have come to expect,' I said. 'While we are prepared to pay for the meal you have just served, we have to leave.'

'And that goes for me too,' said Eric, jumping up. 'You'll settle up, won't you, Ernie?' And with that he was off out of the place. Through the window we saw him running to catch the bus at the stop on the other side of the road.

Nor do I think anybody had warned Joan that her Eric was probably the most difficult man in the world to feed. I had done the catering in the bus-caravan so I know. He can't stand undercooked food. If it's steak it has to be practically burnt. If it's roast beef it has to be cut in thin slices from the outside part. If it's chops, they have to be thin chops. He won't eat fat and he doesn't like chicken. He says he likes fishing but he won't eat fish.

ERIC Nonsense, I'll eat kippers and I'll eat all the Morecambe shrimps you can put in front of me. I'll eat curry and Chinese food provided I'm sure that I'm not being served with cat. I'll eat snails, winkles, crab, lobster, sheep's trotters, pig's belly, black pudding and of course avocado pears.

ERNIE   All of which are so easy, inexpensive and such a pleasure for a loving wife to serve! I was so happy for Joan to do it. Besides, I had some marrying of my own to do and I wasted no time in making Doreen my wife.

DOREEN   We were married on 18 January 1953. My vicar in Peterborough wouldn't marry us on a Sunday, so we wound up having the job done in a Baptist chapel. By that time I had given up show business and was running a dancing school, so we walked out of the chapel under an avenue of tap-shoes held up by my ex-pupils. Eric's mother was there to wish us happiness. Somebody reserved us a compartment on the train to Sheffield—it must have been Ernie's dad; my Ern was never that romantic!— and the engine driver had been tipped off too because he gave a 'Woo-Woo' toot as we steamed out of Peterborough.

I attended the Monday matinee of the pantomime. It was *Dick Whittington* with Ken Platt as the star. Tony Heaton was the Dame —he later committed suicide by walking into the sea at Blackpool —and the boys were Captain and Mate. Ernie had booked a box for me. I can remember watching from there, being terribly embarrassed by Eric who kept looking up at me and smirking. Had it happened a few years later he would probably have stopped the show and announced the event to the audience, and made a big fuss about it, and got a wonderful reaction. But in those days Morecambe and Wise knew their place and kept it.

We were in Sheffield about ten weeks. As Eric and Joan had rented a house for the duration of the show, Ernie thought it would be a good idea if we stayed in the bus-caravan which had been left parked outside my parents' house in Peterborough. On a Saturday night after the show Ernie and I went to Peterborough to fetch it. Our return journey in the bus-caravan began very early on the Sunday morning. To begin with the car battery was low, too low to work the starter-motor, however Ernie eventually managed to get the engine started with the crank handle. After that it wasn't too bad until we were approaching Sheffield when it stopped and wouldn't budge. It was freezing cold and we were at our wits end when a young man came up and offered to give us a hand. It was quite late by this time and our helper was all dressed up and on his way to the cinema. After about an hour of trying to restart the engine, during which Ernie kept reminding him he'd be late for the cinema, he decided he wouldn't bother to go after all and Ernie was so touched by the man's kindness he started to cry. I think the engine felt sorry for us after that because it burst into life.

Ernie now started begging our good Samaritan to accept payment for his kindness, which he refused and Ernie burst into tears again. I could tell you of about a few more tear-jerking occasions, but to cut a long story short we eventually got to a garage at a place called Lodge Moor. There we put it in the car park and there it remained.

It was a very cold winter. There is a picture of the garage with the snow practically up to the sign on a bus stop on the road before it. To get to the bus-caravan we had to walk on piled-up snow that took us above the roofs of cars, but oddly enough there was no snow at all around where we lived. So you can imagine how much we were ribbed about the snow being melted by the heat of our passion, and more besides.

Lodge Moor was high up. They used to say in Sheffield that the wind in that place came straight from Siberia. I remember one night a policeman opening a fan light and shining his lamp in to see if we were alive. We heard him saying, 'Those poor devils in there it must be freezing.'

In fact it was wonderfully cosy, and the only heating we had was one paraffin lamp.

Ernie was always the first to get up in the morning, and he made a cup of tea. He's kept that up ever since. He tells people, 'A good cup of tea first thing puts her in a good mood for the rest of the day!'

As far as I can remember Ernie was never able to start the bus-caravan again, so it was sold in Sheffield. We then bought a brand new Triumph Mayflower for £725 in cash which Ernie paid for out of his savings. We lived in digs when we were on tour and in caravans during pantomimes and summer seasons.

ERNIE If you asked me to name some of the most comfortable and happy places we stayed in on tour, I would say without hesitation theatrical digs, *when they were well run.*

I remember a Miss Davies in Swansea. We would come into

our room to a great roaring fire, so piled up with coal there were holes in the hearth-rug from burning embers. You slept on a feather bed which, believe me, is far more comfortable than any interior sprung mattress, provided it's well tossed every day, as she did ours. She was about seventy and her Christmas dinner was out of this world. We used to take a party of people in the cast who had nowhere to go back with us to Miss Davies' place for Christmas dinner.

DOREEN Christmas can be a thin time for pros, which is something few people realise. Just before Christmas, business can be slack. Those who have not worked may be broke, but they wouldn't normally get paid until after they had done a week's work, and pantomimes either started on Christmas Eve or Boxing Day. Besides, pantomime managements didn't like members of the cast to disperse to their homes for Christmas because there is always the risk of their not being able to return if the weather suddenly closes in with snow. So, in later years, when we took to renting a furnished house for the run of a pantomime we would give a Christmas dinner party for those who didn't have anywhere to go.

ERIC Yes, I remember Miss Davies of Swansea. She was great. But I think the real star of Britain's theatrical landladies must have been Mrs McKay of 11, Daisy Avenue, Manchester. She charged a little more than most of the others, but she was 5-star. She had two semi-detached houses knocked together, one side for variety and the other for the 'legitimate' theatre, and her policy was that never the twain should meet. One year Dame Flora Robson was staying at Mrs McKay's when we were there. Flora went to our show which was at the Hulme Hippodrome, and later she came round to our side at Daisy Avenue to see us, much to our landlady's consternation. I don't know why because both variety and 'straight' theatre people get on very well, I have found. We admire their talent for interpreting character, and they I think admire our ability to register with an audience without the advantage of a plot.

Mrs McKay was always very bill conscious—as Ernie used to add, when she gave you the bill you were conscious of it! Forgive him. Where was I? Ah, yes, Mrs McKay. A star herself in her own right, she paid special deference to the stage stars she catered for. For these there was a private dining room.

ERNIE Like Mrs Coombes at Hagley Road, in Birmingham. She had a private dining room for stars. On one occasion Sir Donald Wolfit was in it, eating in solitary spendour, when part of the ceiling plaster collapsed above his head and landed in his soup.

ERIC You'll hear plenty of stories about landladies who would accommodate their guests in more ways than one. With all due deference to them, I have yet to meet a theatrical landlady who appeared likely to inspire the sort of ideas that give rise to dirty stories. The average was a set, middle-aged matron who generally worked extremely hard. She brought you early morning tea in bed. She might do your laundry for a little extra. She might even throw in a few other personal comforts if your tastes were sufficiently mature to ask for them. But to be honest I don't think I ever encountered one whose moral turpitude ever seemed in doubt.

If anything, it was always the other way about. Hanky-panky between guests was strictly forbidden—'I don't keep a disorderly house!'—and in the days of ration books it was far from easy for an unmarried couple to slip a fast one over an eagle-eyed landlady.

A favourite dodge was, 'Oh I've lost my ration book and we're just eating off my husband's this week.' Or, 'We're faddy about food, so we'll go out and buy the sort of things we want you to cook.'

But many a guilty pair quailed before their landlady's look of severe suspicion. One landlady actually suspected sin between Lilywhite and Doreen although her wedding ring hadn't left her finger from the day he had slipped it on hot from my sweaty waistcoat pocket in that Baptist chapel in Peterborough.

There were landladies who sat up late to make sure nobody brought an unauthorised girl into his room. Comedians had a lecherous reputation—'What do you expect when they can have the pick of the chorus?' was a familiar indictment you heard from those vigilant critics of theatre morals.

There's the classic story of the landlady who suspected a certain well-known comedian of bringing a girl home and took to listening at the bottom of the stairs for his footsteps. Every night she heard only one pair of footsteps, treading a bit heavily but still only one pair—until one night something made her decide to investigate further. She went into the hall to find the comedian creeping up the stairs—carrying a chorus girl on his back.

ERNIE Digs landladies worked hard for the prices they charged. When we first started touring in 1939, it was thirty to thirty-five shillings a week and that included full board—three large meals a day for a breed of guest noted for their large appetites. By the early fifties prices had risen to three pounds ten shillings, but even in the late fifties a fiver was considered pricey.

What every pro looked for was a place where the landlady was just starting out and doing her best to please. Beginners were always good—more attentive and more generous. They carved the meat hot—not cold and then reheated it. They served you with large plates, not small plates to make the helpings look big, and they piled your plate high and not just with potatoes. Yes, they were good, but sadly they caught on soon enough once they realised they had all the regulars they could cope with. Then they became seasoned landladies, business women, who gave exactly what was expected, who made what they could out of a very slender margin of profit, and were good or bad in the way that human nature generally sorts out people into categories in its own way.

ERIC Funnily enough, the worse the digs the stricter the rules and the dirtier and nastier the landlady. I remember a really crummy joint in Wigan where I stayed with Joan and our daughter Gail who was then only four months old. Joan and I slept in a double-bed with a cot by the side of it for Gail. When we got up in the morning, Joan's face was blotched and swollen, and the baby's face was so swollen you could barely see her eyes. I plucked back the bed sheet, and we saw them—horrible, smelly bed-bugs, bloated with blood. I stormed down to the landlady.

I said, 'We're leaving this filthy place. It's riddled with bed-bugs. You ought to see my wife's face and the baby's.'

'Yes, leave,' she said, 'and take your filthy bed-bugs with you. You brought them here. This is a clean house, I'll have you know. Clean and respectable.'

ERNIE You'll note that Eric didn't have a bite on him. At least bed-bugs aren't cannibals! Anyhow, there were other sides to landladies. Some were retired pros and at the drop of a hat could be persuaded to stop serving a meal and go into their act which might become a complete 15-minute spot. Others were difficult enough to get started but that done you found you might have a problem getting them to stop. Arthur Askey used to tell the story of the landlady who had a special party piece which no one had heard because she was too bashful to do it in front of pros. She was a funny old thing, and Arthur, ever on the look out for real-life material, kept on trying to persuade her to do it. In the end she agreed. It was Saturday dinner time; she had just given her guests their soup. When I say she agreed to perform, it was with certain reservations. It had to be from behind the door. Her guests then heard a series of clucks and quacks while their land-lady went through her entire repertoire of farmyard impressions. It went on and on till in the end her starving guests had to go out and beg her to turn it off. Not only that, they next discovered to their horror that the big family dog and got into the kitchen and wolfed back most of the meat on the plates.

ERIC A perk landladies used to have, especially in places like Blackpool where they were in a position to recommend shows to their patrons, was a free ticket to the opening night or dress rehearsal of every new show.

Some of these women took show business so desperately seriously that not only were they capable of putting their residents right off going to a particular show, but they also made their disapproval clear to any of the cast who happened to be staying with them. Bill Burke, an old comic we knew, told us of the time he first played Morecambe. On the first night he 'died the terrible death'—he didn't get any laughs at all. As if that wasn't bad enough, when he got back to his digs the landlady said, 'There's no supper for you tonight. You were bloody awful.'

ERNIE Worse happened to Harry Secombe. In his famous shaving routine Harry gets pushed on to the stage. He apologises for being late, says he hasn't had time to shave, and then proceeds, with a blunt razor, to do a very funny take-off in mime of the different ways in which people shave. He was playing Bolton, but instead of laughs he got a sort of lynch-mob murmuring that ended with a slow hand-clap.

When he came off the stage, the theatre manager came up to him and said, 'You're not shaving in my time,' and fired him. But the final blow came from his landlady when he got back to his digs. 'You're not staying in my house,' she said. 'You can get the first train in the morning.'

A feature of every theatrical digs was the visitor's book, and it was usually interesting to turn back the pages and see the names of people, some of them famous, who had stayed there years before. Everyone was asked to write in it and naturally expected to say something complimentary in the remarks column. This wasn't always easy, however pros had got round the problem of committing themselves to any false praise they may have to give. A code had evolved rather like the signs tramps used to leave on hedgerows to indicate the generosity or otherwise of a certain housewife. There is no harm now in revealing the secret of the remarks-column code as the days of touring in variety are over. You could write all the eulogies you liked in a visitors' book, but if you did not intend them to be taken seriously you merely added, 'And I shall certainly tell my friends.' That was the thumbs-down signal. Whenever we saw those words we groaned. They were never wrong.

9

Eric On Sunday 13 September 1953, my wife Joan started to give birth to our first child. We were at my parents' place in Morecambe.

'How long is the process going to take?' I asked the midwife when she called that morning full of bustle and the usual business about hot water. It was like the sort of birth-scene cliché you used to see in films.

'Oh, it'll be here by twelve.'

'Twelve what?'

'Noon, of course,' she said. 'I can tell. I'm seldom wrong, you know.'

'What's it going to be?'

'A boy, definitely. I have a way of knowing.'

'Oh. You wouldn't care to let me into the secret?'

Her reply was a coy giggle as she tripped out of the house with a little squeak from her low-heeled shoes and took off on her bike with a basket on the carrier at the back.

Joan had not been very well during her pregnancy, particularly during the first three months. Part of that time we were up in Sheffield in *Dick Whittington*. Sheffield is a fine city now, but twenty years ago it was grim, and in winter it was perpetually wrapped in smog. I used to send Joan to Morecambe or Margate where the sea air immediately made her feel better, but the moment she returned to Sheffield she was as bad as ever. Pantomime is hard on wives. Joan and Doreen would be stuck with Ernie and me in a smelly dressing-room from about eleven-thirty in the morning on matinee days till past midnight.

Then the touring began with those endless Sunday train journeys and dreary changes, and at the end of them digs. Some good—Joan still sends Christmas cards to landladies whose kindness she has never forgotten. But others were terrible. Now at last the nine months had passed and I waited for twelve noon.

By twelve midnight the promised boy hadn't shown up. I was nervous and jittery. By midday, another twelve hours later, *he* was still an unfulfilled promise, and by now I had developed a distinct twitch.

It was the year we were at the Winter Garden Theatre in Blackpool with Alan Jones as top of the bill. Blackpool was twenty-seven miles away. We didn't own a car which meant I had to leave the house in the early afternoon to get to Blackpool in time.

We were on the stage in the middle of our first spot when I noticed the MD making signs at me. I looked again and saw him clearly mouth the words, 'IT'S A GIRL.'

As we came off the stage, the stage-manager was there to confirm it. My mother had telephoned the news. It was a girl weighing six pounds. I was given permission to leave the theatre before the finale.

When the cast were all lined up after the curtain calls, Alan Jones stepped forward. 'Ladies and gentlemen, I have an announcement to make. You'll notice that Eric Morecambe of Morecambe and Wise, that wonderful double-act on the bill, was not with us for the finale. Well, folks, there's a good reason. He's rushing home this very minute to his wife because he has just become the father of a *six month* baby girl.'

Those, I am told, were his very words. Jack, his son, who was in the audience that night, may remember them.

Alan gave Gail her first present—£5 which went into a Post Office savings account we opened in her name. George and Alfred Black, who were presenting the show, sent Joan an enormous bouquet of flowers. More and more flowers started to arrive till the bath and all the buckets and vases in the house were filled with them. There was a whip-round by the cast and they bought Gail a high-chair.

So our lives changed, and I came face to face with a major reality in life. I had to learn to drive a car. Before this I had left Ernie to cope with the driving.

Now, don't get me wrong. I had faced up to my responsibilities practically from the time Joan began to look worried a couple of months after we were married. HP hadn't been invented in those days, at least not for rogues and vagabonds of the variety theatre who were here today and gone tomorrow. So we saved, which was something I'd never been able to do previously. By the time Gail arrived we were in a position to buy a car, which we did, though I confess I didn't nor ever did know the make.

Through a miracle, and because the instructor had liked us at the Winter Garden, having been at the theatre on the night of Alan Jones' announcement, I was able to give him a big spiel about Joan and the baby and our having to drive down to Margate for the christening, and passed my driving test. My unconscious hope had been that he would fail me. When he didn't, I panicked.

He handed me a chit. 'You can take down your L plates,' he said.

'What do I put up instead?—B for Beware?'

He laughed. 'I don't advise taking part in the Monte Carlo Rally just as yet, but you'll be all right.'

My first solo drive back to Joan was an ordeal by fear. To get from Morecambe to Margate was going to be the next. I wrote to the AA, asking for a route that would get us there by using only B roads which I felt would be quieter and safer. In those days the AA sent you detailed routes. The one I received must have taken their entire routes department a week to compile—it ran to sixty-three pages. The journey took us two days with an overnight stop at Huntingdon, and when we got there it took at least four minutes for Joan to prise my hands with their stark-white knuckles loose from the steering wheel.

It's funny, we did not go near Huntingdon again until quite recently when we formed a company with Joan's brother and bought a pub called the Tudor at Fenstanton, which is near

Huntingdon. Taking heart, we have gone even a stage further, and bought the Golden Lion, a hotel at St Ives, also near Huntingdon.

At one place on that epic journey we even took a ferry—another terror-filled obstacle with people behind honking and a nurse coming up and asking if I was feeling all right. Still, we did go through some beautiful parts of England and we made Margate in time for the christening—in the church in which we had been married.

Now comes the next stage in our progress as a family. I have mastered the car, an enormous advantage when you're touring with a young baby who has to be breast-fed every four hours and requires a boot full of luggage, not to mention baskets, buckets, a carry-cot—I won't go on; the list still gives me a twitch. But this is only at the beginning. Soon the baby must have a pram, besides a push-chair, the high-chair and God knows what else. Further, you're back in Sheffield, in a rented house on a hill, during another bitterly cold winter with a Wuthering Heights wind whistling down the chimneys, blowing smoke back into the unheated rooms, and you're coming home at midnight starving and wanting a meal, and your wife has to be up again at six to feed the baby. That's when you start thinking, as I did. The answer suddenly hits you straight between the eyes—a caravan.

It was a Paladin Nomad sixteen-footer, a beautiful white thing. It was bought in London and towed up to Sheffield by Stan Stennett, who was topping the bill in the pantomime and was a very good friend. Stan, a born caravanner, was the one who had recommended the Paladin. He showed me how to couple it and uncouple it and bring down the legs so that it stood firmly on the ground.

I loved our Paladin. Everything about it was so cosy, so cleverly designed. I am not the neatest person in the world, but being in that caravan inspired me to hang up clothes instead of leaving them on the floor, and to stow things away properly.

When the pantomime ended we decided to take the Paladin down to Margate. Naturally I was nervous. I would have to do all the towing myself; Joan didn't drive at the time, and in any case had her hands full with the baby—Gail was a handful from the day she was born.

So we set out, terrified of getting a scratch on our new pride and joy. Now, towing a caravan is far from straightforward. In fact, it is extremely complicated, and Stan, who had once driven articulated lorries for a removals firm, had never for a moment imagined that I would need to be initiated into the mysteries.

At first it was deceptively simple. We were going in a forward direction on a level road bowling along very nicely though slowly. We were beginning to congratulate ourselves when we came to a steep hill which started getting steeper and steeper and steeper. I could feel the engine hurting a little. The gears were on the steering column. I changed down from fourth to third, which helped for about ten yards. The engine was hurting again so I whipped it down into second. No help. Down into first, but the car had stopped and was going backwards.

Bear with me in this because at the time I didn't know that while a car with a caravan may go forwards in the way you expect, in reverse it behaves ridiculously. Take my word for it. In seconds we were jack-knifed across the road, in the centre of a terrifying orchestra of blaring horns as cars and lorries slammed past on either side.

I shouted at Joan—I don't remember what I said, but she has never forgiven me for it. And I stood on the brakes.

Leaping out of the car with the baby in her arms, she frantically started flagging down the traffic. They had stopped anyway, an impatient line rapidly forming up and down the road.

I tried to back off the middle of the road, but the situation kept getting worse. Then a driver from one of the cars took over the backing operation. He got us to one side, practically into the hedgerow, scratching the Paladin's beautiful white paint, though at that stage I wouldn't have minded if a tree had fallen on it.

'Let the engine cool down,' the man said, lifting up the bonnet. Then, shouting, 'NO, DON'T TOUCH THE RADIATOR CAP!'

I jumped back.

'It's boiling,' he said.

'Oh.'

'Now calm down. Have a cup of coffee, smoke a cigarette, and in half an hour the engine should start again. Go up the hill in bottom gear. OK?'

'OK.'

'Say, weren't you in that pantomime at Sheffield?'

'Yes.'

'I thought so. Anyway, good luck.'

'By the way,' I said, 'you wouldn't like to buy the caravan?—I'll throw in the wife and kid as well.'

He smiled. 'You'll feel better when it's over, you may even laugh about it one day.' And he was gone.

Eventually we got up the hill, found a caravanserai and stopped for the night. Two days later we crawled into Margate, our marriage practically on the rocks.

JOAN The caravan saga had only begun. My turn for adventure came when I put a casserole in the oven. After a while I noticed that the Calor gas jets had gone out. Thinking I'd better relight it, I struck a match and opened the oven door. There was a hot white flash and a bang as I was thrown violently backwards.

The baby was in a carry-cot on wheels near the oven. Instinctively I looked round for her. The carry-cot had been flung against the rear of the caravan. I took her out—she was all right. Then I felt my head burning—my hair was on fire. I slapped it out, catching a glimpse of my face in a mirror. It was black. I looked closer to find my eyebrows were gone.

A man standing a hundred yards off had heard the explosion. He came running and I greeted him screaming. 'My casserole! Look at my casserole!'

ERIC A good title for a song! As you can see, we had to learn to adapt ourselves to gipsy life, especially in a Northern city during the winter with nowhere to park the caravan, no sanitary arrangements, no running water and a pile of dirty nappies. Under such conditions caravanning was penitential—it played havoc with my nerves, and my driving. I remember in Manchester trying to park between two cars when Joan wanted me to stop outside a chemist's shop. There was a sudden banging on my window—I was being welcomed by the irate owner of a brand new car into which I had backed the caravan.

There followed a nightmare of a double-act, examining the damage and exchanging names and addresses in icy rain—crosstalk (forgive the pun) in which the car owner got all the bitter laughs.

JOAN   On the other hand, caravanning had its moments. Our first summer season together in Blackpool was glorious. Nothing but sunshine. We were parked in the grounds of a holiday camp, in a section fenced off for theatrical people, and we lived in swimsuits. We had access to a lovely swimming pool where we would spend the entire day.

It was the year Eric decided to have a 'serious stab at fishing' which was the way he put it. He found three boys in the theatre orchestra with the same idea and they planned to go out early one Sunday. Eric was to pick them up at six so he went to bed straight after the show the previous night. I was instructed to set the alarm but not to worry, he would get his own breakfast.

The next I knew I was being shaken awake by Eric.

'You've let me down. You didn't set the alarm. I've overslept.'

'Sorry,' I said, 'but I am sure I set it.'

'Well, you didn't.'

'Can I get you anything?'

'No.'

He was frantically pulling on waders and other gear between spoonfuls of cereal and cold milk. As he was about to dash out, I noticed the time. It wasn't two o'clock in the morning.

'Look again at the clock,' I said.

He picked it up. 'Oh hell, I am a fool. Sorry for blowing up. Look, there's no point in my getting undressed again. I'll lie down fully clothed and snatch a nap before the alarm.'

Unfortunately he had turned off the alarm when he picked up the clock. I next awoke with the sun streaming in and Eric still asleep—at 8.30.

'What shall I do? I told them I'd meet them at six. I've let them down.' He was flapping.

'Why not go and see,' I suggested.

He did. They were still waiting, being fishermen, and they went out and had a wonderful day catching nothing.

Today, Gail is a calm, sweet-natured girl. But at nearly two she was in mischief the whole time, never wanting to go to bed, never sleeping through the night, never giving me a minute's peace.

There was a children's playground attached to the holiday camp. One day she wanted to go on the swings. I said no, they were too crowded, and in a fit of blind temper she pulled away from me and ran straight for them. Before I could stop her, she had run into a swing with a big child in it. It was coming down, and hit her in the face and sent her flying.

I rushed her to a doctor's surgery. I was in a desperate state thinking she would be disfigured for life, but luckily she wasn't hit full in the face; just on one side. Eric was at work. As the day wore on and I waited for him to return she looked as though she had just gone ten rounds with a fairground bruiser. Poor Eric, his heart nearly broke when he saw her.

She was a mess for quite a time, and I remember getting some dreadful old-fashioned looks from people who, I am sure, thought she had been battered by her parents. We have photographs of her taken at a garden fête with Alma Cogan and Joan Regan. In them Gail is only in profile, looking lovely; the camera couldn't see the other side was black and blue. Luckily her face healed, except that she has just one little spot that never seems to get sunburned when she goes away on holiday. It stays pale.

After that summer we towed the caravan to a field in More-cambe, where a farmer allowed us to park it for a small rent. There it remained for the next nine months—we were finding it easier by now to travel by car and stay in digs. Besides, we had plans for a more permanent home of our own. So we sold the caravan. It was nice to see the look of sheer relief on Eric's face when he knew he would never have to tow it again.

ERNIE Life was simpler for Doreen and myself. We didn't have a family. When we first married we began a home for ourselves in a back room in Doreen's parents' house in Peterborough. Doreen asked her mother if she'd mind if we bought a few sticks of furniture.

'No, that's all right,' she said, 'so long as you can get it all in that one room.'

The first thing we bought, I remember, was a bedside cabinet. Then came a wardrobe and drawers. We have them still.

I have always felt financially insecure because everything about our profession is so impermanent. I know people at the top, stars making thousands, yet they are worried out of their minds at the thought that it could stop tomorrow and they would have to start selling off what they have got in order to live.

One answer to the question of your future is insurance. I remember a fellow called Jack Kevil was after me to take out a policy. He persisted, like a good insurance man, and in the end I said yes, and I took out an endowment policy for £350 with profits for twenty years. It cost me £11 a year; I felt I could afford that. It matured quite recently, and I dropped Jack a line saying, 'Well, I think I can now afford to retire!'

In the 'fifties, I also took out a pension policy—it cost me £15 a year. In those days we were never sure, Eric and I, where the next week's work was coming from. No pro could be sure. It may have been an over-pessimistic view, but it was this more than anything which made us accept everything that came our way. It got to the point where were were working all the time too scared to tell our agent it was time we had a holiday.

The first house Doreen and I bought was in Peterborough, next to an old windmill. We had it built by a local firm and it cost £2,850, which was cheap for a detached, three-bedroomed house with a fine lounge and large garden. I took out a mortgage for thirty years because I felt that if I was all washed up or ill I could just about manage the repayments. At the end of the first year I realised that only £24 had come off the capital borrowed on the house, so I smartly upped the amount I had to pay. I wish I still had that place. It must be worth a tidy sum.

Then, about fifteen years ago, the man I rented caravans from suggested I bought a nice piece of land near his house. He said I didn't have to build on it for two years but that it could be a good investment.

Well, I bought it, and Doreen and I wound up by building our dream house on it which we designed from a series of pictures in a magazine. When we applied for planning permission, the Council said there was too much fenestration (too many windows) and the roof didn't slope enough. They also objected to the green tiles we wanted. Well, we have since seen houses in and around

Peterborough with more fenestration, and flatter and greener roofs, but no matter. We're happy with it now the way it is. There's an open-plan lounge with stairs coming down into the room, and a Cotswold stone fireplace. There's a sapele floor (it looks like basket work) with electric under-floor heating and a nautical bar at the back. There are three bedrooms upstairs. The garden is huge but we have a gardener who keeps it in trim—at one stage we used to have to go from Blackpool to Peterborough every week-end just to mow the lawn and thrash the weeds.

It is the place to which we will probably one day retire, but at the moment we use it only for week-ends. Most of our work is now in London, so during the week we live in a second house we have, at Harrow. For holidays we have the Malta flat Eric has mentioned, and for the river during the summer, and even sometimes at Christmas, we have a thirty-foot cabin cruiser moored on the Norfolk Broads.

But I've jumped a few years and skipped a part of our lives that I think is interesting. Namely pantomime. During those early years, pantomime kept us busy for twelve difficult and expensive winter weeks. It was solid bread and butter but it sometimes meant virtually living in crummy dressing-rooms. I should add that many of the variety theatres we played in had become really decrepit backstage. In the dressing rooms you'd find cracked mirrors, old wardrobes with no hangers, springs sticking out of the settee and filthy carpets, if any carpet at all. Which reminds me of one dressing room that was so bad that Eric was prompted to write on the wall, by the side of the mirror:

> *I was here a week.*
> *Oh Lord, what fame is it we seek*
> *That led me up this ruddy creek?*
>
> E.M.

A year later we were back at the same theatre, in the same dressing-room. Under Eric's graffiti were the lines:

> *O foolish jester, learn your craft.*
> *The clown must cry that others laugh.*
> *Seek not cushions, chairs to size,*
> *Sack your partner Ernie Wise!*
>
> E.S.

At the start of a pantomime, Doreen and Joan would set about making our dressing-room cosy and attractive. Curtains appeared on the windows, frilly loose covers on the furniture, framed photographs on the dressing table. And for our other needs, an electric kettle, frying pan and pressure cooker, and a chest full of packets and tins of goodies.

The snag about pantomime, as far as I was concerned, was that you invariably had to rehearse in drill halls with no heating, so that by the time the show started everyone in the cast was down with bad chests and flu. I invariably had sinus trouble and would go on the stage drugged up to the eyes. Besides, the unnatural hours you kept in the theatre during the matinees, from midday till past 11.30 at night, breathing the same air, could not have been good for you. All you had of the sun was about ten minutes in the morning on your way to the theatre. Your wife would start cooking your main meal at about eleven, which meant you didn't get to bed before one o'clock. It was like working a twelve-hour afternoon and night shift.

Doreen spent a lot of time with me in dressing-rooms, more so, naturally, than Joan did with Eric once Gail came. Early on we messed together, but later when we got separate rooms we ate separately, which of course was more convenient when we both had different sets of relatives and friends calling.

ERIC   We had to make our own fun backstage, otherwise life would have been impossible. Remember those things called poo-poo cushions which made a very vulgar sound when you sat on them? I once brought in a few of these. Consternation and red faces all around. In one of the pantomimes I was a robber. For most of the time I wore nothing but a big cloak. Under this I could secrete a poo-poo cushion, and on the stage with Stan Stennett I was able to give him a very controlled reply from a poo-poo cushion under my arm before speaking my lines. I have seen him crying with laughter with the audience not knowing what it was all about, which I know is very wrong.

During matinees we went even further. With an audience of OAPs, all asleep and waiting only for you to sing *On Mother Kelly's Doorstep* and for the Dame to lift up her dress and show her big red bloomers for the big laugh, I would let Stan have some very broad ones from behind the backcloth. Or, when the Princess came on, in deference to her position, some pert little sounds.

Once we had a big-time producer named John Beaumont coming to visit Stan backstage. Before his arrival, Ernie and I planted half a dozen poo-poo cushions in Stan's dressing-room. We tried them out in every vantage position so that no matter where the great man sat he would bring forth the vulgar melody we were praying for. Ernie and I waited, listening outside the door. There wasn't a note. John Beaumont hadn't bothered to sit down at all.

A Dame in one of the pantomimes was Eddie Malloy. Eddie was a fantastic Dame, but a Dame who hated no part more because he loathed doing female impersonations. I have never seen anything like it. If a matinee started at 2.15, an hour before that every Dame in the business would be putting on his girdle, stockings, bloomers, bra, make-up and the rest of it. Not Eddie. He would still be in the nearest betting shop at 2.05 placing bets, after which Eddie would dash into the theatre, throw on his costume and be in the wings with time enough to spare to start hating the part before he went on.

Eddie's passion was gambling and under his guidance we won quite a bit of money—on our first race our syndicate took £120. We got to the point where we were able to organise our exits and entrances so that we could watch the finish of every race on TV. Eddie infected the entire cast with his gambling fever. To my knowledge everybody's account was up by the end of the season.

JOAN Eric used to bring Eddie home on Sundays, which was fine. But in winter you are ruled more or less by the weather, and when you are married, as I am, to one of the greatest worriers alive, his worries and nervous twitchings and whatever else become very catching. What Eric was always afraid of was that it might snow, so much so that if a single white fleck appeared outside the window there was consternation. There were times when these week-ends scarcely seemed worth it.

ERIC After that pantomime we didn't see Eddie again for at least seven years. Then one evening Joan and I were at a show in

London, sitting in the second row of the stalls, when who should walk on, playing the part of a smart music hall type, but Eddie Malloy. I fell about laughing before he even opened his mouth. He looked down astonished, immediately recognised me and he was finished for the rest of the show.

I watched out for him after that. If you look off at certain times in a show you can anticipate a particular entrance; and there among the cracks and joins in the scenery, I would see Eddie's eye looking through at us. I knew he knew that I was going to laugh the moment he spoke his lines. I knew he was almost dreading coming out—he wanted laughs, of course, but not the sort of belly stuff he was getting from me. It was the best fun I've had for many a year. Joan and I went backstage to see him later, a great teddy bear of a man, and I apologised for causing him embarrassment. He just laughed.

Going back to our early days in pantomime, Joan and I soon had to decide on the sort of home life we would make for ourselves and our children. Show business creates problems that don't exist for people outside it. This was brought home to me one day when Joan came backstage with Gail and a couple of chorus girls started making a fuss over the child. It happened at Swansea. They took her off to their dressing room. When we saw her next they had made her up with lipstick and rouge, and a beauty spot. Gail was in her element, and I had a vision at that moment of the possibility of her growing up as a showbiz child, spoilt and precocious, and seeing and having too much of life too soon, and I put an immediate block on her being brought backstage after that.

She would be a normal child, have a normal home life and a normal schooling. Joan was in total agreement.

Before long we decided to have a second child. Where Gail had come as a complete surprise, we actually planned Gary. Then, once Joan started carrying Gary, we went to stay at the Torrington Arms, a pub that her brother and her people have at North Finchley. His wife and young family were there too so there was always company for her when I was away touring. We remained based there until we bought an old Victorian house, converted it into two flats, and moved into the downstairs one. We sold the upstairs one to a charming old lady, Miss Belcher, who still lives there. I remember Gary was at the crawling stage when we moved into this, our first permanent home.

Before that we were nomads and part of this nomadic period was spent in Blackpool. It was an important time in our lives.

10

E<small>RIC</small> Let's get Blackpool in its right perspective. To begin
with let's look at it. To its everlasting glory it is in Lancashire.
They (and *they* include E. Wise) can never take *that* away from it.
I know that it may have suffered in recent years because more
people are going abroad for their holidays but in the early 'fifties
Blackpool was a veritable mecca.

On a fine day you could see our audiences all at once. You
merely had to stand on a pier and look down on the sands in
either direction. One thought that often struck me was My God,
if a gull was flying overhead and actually tried to miss somebody it would have been a miraculous feat. I have seen swarms
of humanity in many places but seldom anything to compare
with those masses seething in an infinite permutation of meaning-
less activity that normally sober and industrious people occupy
themselves with during their annual holiday. And yet, if any
one of these nature lovers—and the English are noted for wanting
to get away from it all—had but gone a mile or two out of the
town of Blackpool on either side, where the sand is equally soft
and white, he would not have encountered a soul.

Anyhow, with a population of a million people during the
high season, Blackpool could support more live theatre shows
than any other resort in Britain, besides cinemas, nightclubs, the
Golden Mile with its glaring lights, side shows and occasional

punch-ups; and some excellent eating places all over the town. In some you could order oysters with champagne which you could buy by the glass.

There were press promotions schemes, beauty competitions, show business cricket and football matches, big functions such as the Mayoral Garden Party and the famous Water Rats Ball, and the ceremonial switching on of the lights as an extra boost to the season that brought in its wake unbelievable traffic jams with everything and everybody trying to move in one direction and not apparently succeeding. And invariably, as if the rain god resented the lights, there followed a monsoon of howling gales.

It was a long season, from the beginning of April until mid-October, enlivened by a show business community that was large and gay but with a conscious sense of precedence in which your standing was established not just by your position on the bill but by the sort of theatre in which you were playing.

At the top of the league was the Opera House with its magnificent spectacular shows and beautiful sets and scenery. After that, and I don't suggest this is any sort of descending scale, came the Hippodrome (later the ABC Theatre); the Palace, a variety theatre; the Tower, a circus where Charlie Caroli reigned supreme; the Winter Garden; the Central, South and North Piers; the Queens; and the Grand where they presented plays.

In those days, a pro couldn't miss in Blackpool. What with the regular employment, high wages and no travelling expenses, many bought new cars. There were some who became so intoxicated by the laughs of the whelks and belch audiences, who will applaud anything, as to take up such pastimes as golf and flying. Ernie tried both. He gave up flying after two lessons at £1 an hour, and golf after losing three balls costing one shilling and ninepence each. He found it more economical to take Doreen on picnics of flasks of coffee and meat paste sandwiches.

He and Doreen have a story about me, but I shall get in my version before either tries to scoop it. The facts are that one year I rented a house, and arrived there in advance of the family. It was a rambling affair, full of draughts and eerie noises. I would be wakened up in the middle of the night by wind rattling the

PALACE Walthamstow

Phone: LAR 3040

Manager: VIC BROOKER

BOX OFFICE OPEN 10 a.m. to 10 p.m.

| 6-30 | Monday, March 8th, 1948
And during the Week   TWICE NIGHTLY | 8-30 |

GALA NIGHT, WEDNESDAY, 2ND HOUSE

Your Host of the Jazz Club

HARRY PARRY

AND HIS SEXTETTE
WITH JEAN BRADBURY

| VIC WISE & NITA LANE | PIM AND WYN | ASTOR AND RENE |

VIC WISE & NITA LANE
THE WEAK GUY AND HIS WEAKNESS

PIM AND WYN
Comedy Trampoline Act

ASTOR AND RENE
" Have a Go, Joe "

TOMMY WESTWOOD
A Song, A Smile and a Piano

MORECAMBE & WISDOM
JUST TWO GUYS

Archæological find circa 1947. Variety had begun to die

On Waikiki beach, just outside Blackpool. With Doreen (*left*), Gail,
Gary and Joan

With Alma Cogan and Ken Platt at Morecambe

With wives and disappointed audiences

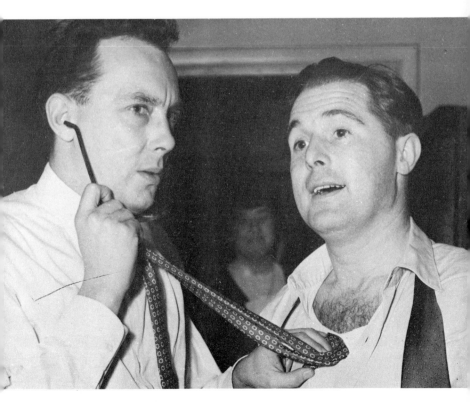

Testing radioactivity—in his wallet

With Teddy boys Kenneth Carden and Teddy Johnson in the
Winifred Atwell TV show

Let's have fun—and you could under the Central Pier, Blackpool

Luton F.C. Junior Reserves. Those booked include Stennett, Cooper, Warriss, Chester, Baker, Matthews and Jewel. Morecambe didn't see the fluorescent ball and Wise sold favours in the stalls

Ernie voting for himself

Wives asking Ernie for money

The pre-Australia problem and Sadie who solved it

Eric's on the right

Having fun at Elbow beach, Bermuda . . .
And working with Ed Sullivan to pay for it

windows, but when I complained about the wind the next morning people would look at me in blank astonishment.

'What wind? The night was hot and airless.'

Hello, hello, what's this 'ere? Something's amiss. Not that I minded the wind—well, let's say I could have stood it. But not the next eerie act on the bill. I woke in the middle of the night to feel a presence in the room. Then, and I am not mistaken, an ice-cold hand stroked my brow. I lay paralysed by the touch, but the moment I was free of it I dived under the bedclothes and shivered with fright for the rest of the night.

Next day I made enquiries. The house had been part of a convent. People had seen the ghost of a nun in black who walked the stairs and passages. That was enough for me. The following night I got a camp bed and went round to Ernie and Doreen's place. I slept in the bathroom. I don't dig ghosts.

Blackpool was a phenomenon. There was nothing like it anywhere else in the world. Blackpool Football Club even had the twilight of Stanley Matthews who, when he was not training, used to play soccer with an old tennis ball in his back yard with a bunch of kids. To his last match Sir Stan remained a gentleman, a player who never wilfully committed a foul. I used to go to watch him when Blackpool played home matches.

Most of the show business crowd met every day at the Savoy or the Winter Garden restaurant for morning coffee and gossip. There'd be at least seventy acts at either place. And there were others I could name who went around the corner to Joe's where you didn't have to tip the waitress.

Arthur Haynes might walk up. 'Hi, boys.'

'Oh, hello, Arthur. Come and sit down.'

Then perhaps Freddie Frinton, or Alma Cogan, or Harry Secombe, or Norman Vaughan, or Ken Platt, or Harry Worth. . . .

Somebody else might pass by. 'Hullo Eric, Ernie. You boys were great last night. I think somebody heard a laugh!'

'Ha ha,' we'd bellow, pretending the gibe was the best joke we'd heard whereas in fact it had a ring of grim truth, and bitter sounding too if Harry Worth was there.

Harry was on the same bill as ourselves at the Winter Garden in 1953. Harry was a ventriloquist, not a great one in our opinion but sort of funny. Never for a moment did we consider a vent as being in opposition to ourselves.

At the start of the show, I remember Alfred Black saying, 'Now boys, we have faith in you. You are going to do well, we know it. This is the very theatre in which Jewel and Warriss got their big break. Now go out there and hit them between their eyes.'

We went out there. I think we must have hit them too hard because they let us have it back where it hurt. We died the death and it happened night after night. Yet at the same time Harry Worth was going from strength to strength, getting brilliant notices about himself in the local paper which he read avidly while we pretended we hadn't even opened the 'rag'—we had, of course, and shut it immediately, not having found anything about ourselves in it.

Now, suddenly, Harry wasn't just a vent we could patronise, he was the cause of anxiety. We had to pull our socks up, revitalise our material. We did and that helped a bit. Anyhow, the show ended.

Three months later who should we meet but George and Alfred Black, who said, 'Harry Worth, my God, that fellow is funny.'

'What do you mean, *funny*. He's a vent.'

'Oh, he's given up being a vent. He's a comic now. He's got an idea for a nervous, bumbling character, and he'll paralyse you.'

We smiled thinly. Our day was ruined. Anyhow we did get a laugh on Harry when we were again on the same bill, at the Derby Hippodrome with Issy Bonn topping it. Harry offered Joan and me a lift from North Finchley which we were very glad of.

Came Tuesday, and Harry was the first out to get the local paper for the write-up. I remember it went something like this: 'Morecambe and Wise were their usual selves (whatever that meant). As for Harry Worth, he may become a comedian one day when he loses his nervousness.' Harry was livid. The critic had missed the whole point of his brand of comedy which was his bumbling nervousness. That write-up made our day!

ERNIE We went to Blackpool for alternate seasons on the advice of our agent, Frank Pope. I loved playing in Blackpool.

126

There was always something happening there to make life interesting. As for practical jokes, one of the funniest I remember was when we got hold of a life-sized ventriloquist's dummy and put it in the pro's loo at the Central Pier—there was only one loo backstage for everybody. We pulled down the dummy's trousers and in the first hour or so several girls backed out with red faces. It wasn't long before we guessed there was one girl who was really bursting to go—after about her third attempt we heard her saying to the others that she suspected the 'person' in the toilet was really somebody's idea of a joke.

Promptly we whipped the dummy out and Eric went in and waited. The girl with the anxious bladder tried again. Eric let her open the door, then gave an 'Oops!' which sent her flying back to their dressing-room.

After a while Eric knocked on the door and called the girl's name.

'Yes?'

'The coast is clear, darling.'

'I'll kill you!' she said.

The North Pier was Blackpool's penitential pier. It stretched out half-way to the Isle of Man and took the brunt of the gales that came from the sunsets over Eric's Morecambe Bay. On a clear day you could see the ocean, on a windy day you were in it. In the girls' dressing room, if one girl attempted to spray lacquer on her hair, it landed on her neighbour's. Spit is often used in theatrical make-up, but you didn't dare spit against the wind that buffeted us through the nooks and crannies of that howling outpost of the entertainment empire. Only the most intrepid ventured the half-mile or so to the theatre, bent double against the wind; only the hardy and fit reached it to occupy their seats. There were casualties on the North Pier. Matt Munro was blown on to one of the deckchairs and broke his arm besides losing his watch through the slats between the deck planking.

There was only one matinee a week, so in fine weather you could spend most of the day sun-bathing. One year, one of the acts on our bill at the Central Pier was The Three Duces. One of them, a Canadian called Paul, persuaded Dennis Spicer's wife to let him have a ride on a big black stallion she had bought.

She said, 'Better not, Paul. He's been fed on nothing but oats and he's as wild as they come.'

'Darling, listen, there isn't a horse that doesn't know I'm master the moment I get on its back,' he assured her.

'Be it on your own head, then.'

'Leave it to me, darling,' he assured her.

She was holding the horse under Central Pier. Paul took the reins and swung into the saddle. Well, I've seen horses go, but never anything like that horse as it shot straight through the crush of humanity on Blackpool beach, a path clearing before it like magic. It shot over windbreaks and rows of deckchairs, over sandcastles with dads half buried under them, over girls undressing, showing as much as they modestly could and old gentlemen watching them through spy-holes in their newspapers, over smart-alecs combing brilliantined hair and girls with radios whose bathing suits never got wet, over harassed mothers with picnic baskets, over old ladies who put on their glasses to see what had momentarily passed, saw nothing and promptly fell asleep.

The horse streaked under the North Pier where Paul was nearly swiped off its back. It went up on the promenade, then along the tramtracks, and was last seen disappearing towards the North Shore.

Meanwhile the show was due to start and Paul had ten minutes to appear on the stage. Consternation. But, as in all situations in the theatre, problems sort themselves out. The bill was rearranged so that by the time Paul finally returned and slid off his mount's back, scarcely able to stand and the horse drenched with sweat, he was able to stagger on to the stage and give a limp performance.

ERIC By this time we were becoming fairly well known on Northern radio. After our fledgling efforts in 1942, supported by our over-enthusiastic studio audience from *Strike a New Note*, we had graduated to a *Workers' Playtime* broadcast from an engineering firm in Birmingham, and then, in 1951, to a *Variety Fanfare* from Manchester.

A girl named Joy Russell Smith, a BBC radio producer in the London area, had auditioned us for *Variety Bandbox*, the Southern edition of *Variety Fanfare*.

'You sound too much like Jewel and Warriss,' she told us. 'Come back in five years.'

One consolation was that we didn't look like Jewel and Warris! Anyhow, reluctant to wait as long as she said, we persuaded a friend to leak the information that Morecambe and Wise were about to be signed up as the resident comedians of *Variety Bandbox*, hoping it would get to the ears of Ronnie Taylor, producer of *Variety Fanfare*, which it did. The ruse worked. Ronnie promptly booked us for a succession of *Fanfares* which eventually ran into forty-five. After that we went on to doing six of our own series of radio shows from Manchester called *You're Only Young Once*.

When Ronnie became head of Light Entertainment BBC North, the man assigned to produce YOYOs, as these shows became known, was Johnny Ammonds. Johnny is now the producer of our TV shows.

That was one of our busiest periods as we did all these radio shows live from Manchester while touring the country in variety. They were broadcast on Sundays. Most of the sketches were built up from ideas and jokes we supplied. We might decide on say a boxing routine, and spend the week thinking up lines like 'Give him a right cross, followed by a left cross, then send for the Red Cross.' Or 'I fell on my back so many times they put handles on my trunks.' Or 'They sold advertising space on the soles of my feet.'

Then on the Sunday we would drive to Manchester to rehearse and be on the air by seven that night.

Frank Roscoe was our writer—it would be more accurate to say we had a share of him. For oft were the times he'd be working on three scripts, one for us, another for Ken Platt, and a third for Al Read. Oft too were the nights we went to the microphone with mimeographed pages of script that were still wet.

Then in 1954 came our first big chance on TV. You could I suppose say that we were a success on radio and in the niche we had chosen for ourselves in variety. That we were beginning to make an impact. The only accurate barometer of success in show business is the money you make. We were getting around £100 a week joint in Blackpool. We were twenty-eight years old, youngish for that sort of money, so we could congratulate ourselves. But a new, unknown quantity had come on the scene in the few years since we'd become pros. Twenty years before, music hall in Britain and burlesque in America had slugged it out with the cinema, and two distinct patterns of popular entertainment had emerged. In Britain one was the theatre, part of which, variety, had become a family institution; the other, the cinema, had become a habit, and, often enough, an opportunity for snogging and more. Radio, which had really only come into its own during the war, was a wonderful substitute for both. Radio could, in a matter of weeks, create nationally known stars who took to topping variety bills between their radio series. This commanded our immediate respect.

As for TV, at first the programmes were so bad no one looked at them, then when they got better those early 9-inch screens put people off. In show business the pundits were all contemptuous. Despite them, by the 1950s more and more people were looking at television. Names were being made on panel games. TV could not be ignored, so you can imagine our excitement when, after a spot we did for BBC-TV, at the Blackpool Tower Ballroom, Ronnie Waldman, head of BBC-TV Light Entertainment signed us up to do a TV series of our own.

Ronnie said, 'You boys are natural TV material.'

'Really?'

'Yes, I know what I am talking about.'

'We believe you.'

This was wonderful. We were to be catapulted into super-stardom. Within weeks we'd be topping variety bills at £500 a week. Ernie would be able to take out another insurance policy.

Bryan Sears was the producer. He came up to Sheffield, where we were playing in variety, for preliminary talks about the show. We put forward some ideas. These were politely but firmly spiked.

Our problem, we were informed, was that we were 'Northern' comics, that a barrier of prejudice existed separating the North from the South and from Wales, Scotland and Ireland as well. It was even hinted that Ronnie Waldman must be off his rocker. Anyhow, to get us through the barrier we were to have no less than six writers on the show in addition to the voice and person-ality of Alma Cogan as resident singer. Alma had been a big suc-cess in the radio show *Take It From Here*.

We went down to London where Joan and I lived in the caravan parked at Acton to be near the BBC-TV Light Entertainment Studios at the old Shepherds Bush Empire.

We rehearsed. The spots were timed to the second. Ernie bought his first TV set so that Doreen could look at the show without anyone interrupting. Telephones were taken off hooks. Everything was set with everyone's fingers crossed at 9.40 on the evening of Wednesday 21 April, 1954, when we hit the TV screens in our first series, *Running Wild*.

In the theatre there isn't the agony of waiting for a reaction; you are never left in doubt about how an audience feels. You know immediately. On TV all you can do is wait. If you've said anything outrageous there'll be telephone calls. But you never know how you've gone down until the morning papers arrive. When they did, on 22 April, each review felt like a slap in the face with a wet fish.

Like: 'How do two commonplace performers such as these get elevated to the position of having a series built around them? Hogsnorton may scream at them deliriously; an invited audience to the Television Theatre may be bludgeoned into applauding mildly; but for me (and I feel sure the majority of viewers) this was one of the most embarrassingly unfunny evenings I have spent in front of the home screen for some time.'

Or: 'How dare they put such mediocre talent on television?'

Or: 'Definition of the week. TV set—the box in which they buried Morecambe and Wise.'

Or: 'Alma Cogan stood out like a sunflower on a rubbish heap.'

Or: 'Can they develop beyond this? They might if they had a script.'

We were utterly appalled. The show had never had any pre-tensions. It was never intended as anything more than a half-hour of song and nonsense. Why this vitriol?

'We're Northern,' Ernie said. 'That's why. You can't win if you're Northern. It's a different world. Look at Dave Morris, a Northern comic—brilliant. He never made it in the South. Sid Field. He was forty-five before he got past the barrier.'

My mother telephoned from Morecambe. She'd seen some of the notices. 'What the devil are you two playing at? I daren't show my face outside the house. We'll have to move. We'll have to change our name.'

Bob Monkhouse was the blue-eyed TV boy of the British press. I seem to remember that every time we were panned by a paper, Bob got a pat on the head.

Ernie broke out in nervous boils, huge red lumps on the back of his neck that Doreen had to dress with lint and plaster. He still has a scar from one of them, not the boil, the plaster.

After the third show, he said, 'This series will finish us if it goes on. Let's go to Ronnie Waldman and ask him to call the whole thing off. If we can stop it now there's a chance we won't be much worse off than we were before the disaster.'

'Yes,' I agreed.

We went up to Ronnie's office in the old Shepherds Bush film studios.

'Come on in, boys,' he said. 'I know, I've seen the notices.'

'We don't want you to feel that you or the BBC are under any obligation to us,' Ernie said. 'I know we have a contract for six shows. But we wouldn't like to hold you to that.'

'Nonsense, boys. I liked the first show. It had a few rough passages here and there, but we can iron those out.'

'Honestly, Mr Waldman,' said Ernie, 'we feel terrible about it. We're scared to death. If it's all the same to you we'd like to pull out.'

'Not on your life.' he said. 'I'm going to hold you to that contract, not because I'm being bloody-minded or because I can't find anybody else to do me a half-hour comedy series every fortnight—most young comics in Britain would give their right arms for a chance like this. No, I'm doing it because I believe you are first-rate TV comedy material.'

As we were leaving, he called us back. He said, 'Stick it out. I have faith in you.'

ERNIE   At last the series ended. By that time our stock was so low, we were placed fourth on the bill at Ardwick Hippodrome in

Manchester where we next appeared although we were the only act which had ever appeared on TV. What a come-down from our high hopes before the TV series.

Eric said, 'We need a new act with new material—we've been too static up to this. Not only that, let's start putting our own personalities across.'

We got together as we had done at Mrs Duer's place in Chiswick when we had to produce a second spot for an extra £2 a week. This time we completely reconstituted our act.

One of the items in it was what we called our wiggling routine. Pop singers were topping a lot of the bills in those days and the premise was that I would coach Eric in the art of putting himself across as a pop singer.

'If you want to become a big pop star and top the bills and have the girls screaming for you, you'll have to learn to wiggle,' was my opening line.

Eric   Pardon?

Ernie   First, you sing a song—any song. Can you sing *You Take a Pair of Laughing Eyes*?

Eric   Of course.

Ernie   Sing it, then.

Eric would start to sing and I'd say: 'Now start wiggling,' making it sound a little like 'widdling' which is a Northern word for having a pee.

Eric   Pardon?

Ernie   I said, 'Start wiggling.'

Eric   Here?

Ernie   But of course.

Eric   In front of everybody?

Ernie   Naturally.

Eric   But I've never wiggled in front of anybody in my life.

Ernie   Well then, it's time you made a start. Go on, try. Get a hold of yourself.

Eric   That would be difficult.

Ernie   Why?

Eric   It's a question of finding oneself so to speak.

Ernie   What's wrong with you?

133

Eric   I'm too inhibited.
Ernie What's that?
Eric   It means I'm too shy. And so on.

We also introduced a lot of personality material. TV had started the personality cult, so we tried to be more ourselves rather than just two comics telling jokes. To our surprise and joy we clicked. We felt our confidence surging back as we heard the audience responding to us, and we wound up with a standing ovation.

ERIC Yes, it was wonderful. We came off the stage dazed. I walked out of the stage-door dazed, and I trudged dazed to where the caravan was parked. There I woke up with a shock. Joan was dazed too, sitting with the baby in her arms, her hair burnt, her eyelashes singed. It was the night of the big explosion.

11

W *hen they look back on their first TV series, Eric and Ernie are convinced that the damage inflicted by the press was really only noticed by agents and managements. The public appeared unaware of the ripple on the entertainment pond, and once this fact was accepted managements were quick enough to exploit the growing publicity value of TV. On programmes Morecambe and Wise began to be introduced as 'fresh from their brilliantly successful TV series,* Running Wild' *or 'Morecambe and Wise of that brilliant TV series,* Running Wild'. *By Christmas 1954 they were being billed as 'those inimitable TV comedians, Eric Morecambe and Ernie Wise', and beginning to believe it themselves.*

Early in 1956 they were approached to do a few spots in a Commercial TV series starring Winifred Atwell. Nervously they accepted.

'They made us an offer we couldn't refuse!' Eric said. 'Though at one stage Ernie began sitting with a list—another nervous boil.'

Johnny Speight was the writer. He recognised that their brand of humour needed to be interpreted on TV in a special way. Indeed Speight was the first to spot that they were ahead of their time, more so in a sense than the Goons because the boys haven't changed their style all that much since then and they are now 'very contemporary', and at their peak. Speight's scripts were first rate, but it was what they did with them and luck, that did the trick.

ERIC Two big things were going to happen in my life. My wife was going to have our second child and we were getting a second, a do or die chance on TV. Imagine the state of my nerves. I would sit rigid, staring at an object like a 'fool gun-dog' until somebody snapped a finger in front of my face.

We rehearsed with a sense of desperation. It got to the stage where Dickie Leeman, the producer, had to take me aside and say, 'Look, Eric, relax. This is only a TV comedy series. God only knows what you'd be like if you were in Death Row and due for execution the next day.'

'If I'm going to "die", let it be on a stage,' I said.

'That's the talk I like to hear. As long as it gets a laugh on my show.'

Came 21 April 1956, the day of the first show in the series. Joan had been taken to hospital and when I phoned, just before the show started, she was already in labour. I remember, in one of the spots things suddenly started going wrong. In the scene I was supposed to be a reveller going home drunk. I hail a taxi which comes up. Ernie is the driver. I open one door, get into the cab and go straight out through the other door.

'How much?' I ask.

'Ten shillings—*sir*,' says Ernie, a real Commie type.

'OK. But next time don't drive so fast.' And Ernie drives off.

As it happened, the taxi could not be driven on to the set because of exhaust fumes. It had to be pulled on by a rope and pulled off accompanied by sound effects. Everything went fine until the time came for Ernie to 'drive' away. Without thinking, he put the taxi into gear and nothing would move it. To the viewer the idea of the spot had been put across, but it was obvious too that something had gone wrong. There was I 'drunk' waiting for Ernie's exit, and getting desperate—the show was live. I tried ad-libbing and pushing. I then got into the front seat to see if I could help, ad-libbing driving instructions to Ernie with desperate *sotto voce* pleas out of the side of my mouth, which the cameras and microphones picked up, while he was ad-libbing back that he would report me to his union, but replying *sotto voce* that something had gone wrong and for God's sake get them to do something about it.

Meanwhile there were people under the taxi (*out of camera*) tinkering. In the end somebody realised we were in gear, a hand appeared and knocked the gear lever into neutral and we sailed off the set with a gasp of relief.

I thought the show had been interrupted with a 'NORMAL SERVICE WILL BE RESUMED AS SOON AS POSSIBLE'. No, Dickie Leeman, with great presence of mind and instinctive nous for what family audiences liked, had kept the cameras on us.

He came bounding down from the control room, beaming. 'Terrific, boys! That was terrific. Fantastic . . .' and so on.

'But we thought—a catastrophe.'

'No, NO! Just what we want.'

And he was right. We had gone down marvellously well, and it was not the only good thing that happened that night. When I got to the hospital straight from the show, I found Joan with a little object with swollen eyes, wet black hair, tiny hands and a little mouth which made funny sucking movements—Ernie.

ERNIE Now, you know it wasn't me. It was your son, Gary.

ERIC Dickie Leeman was so taken with our ad-libbing under stress in a desperate situation that he made it a feature of the series. In the next show a door refused to open that had to in the script. More panic laughs.

The following week the lid wouldn't come off a jar, and the week after that it was something else. Dickie Leeman was enjoying every moment of it, but before long the idea defeated itself. We began to worry about what the next practical joke would be and we had to ask him to desist. Anyhow, the notices we received during that series did a lot to restore our TV confidence.

By the autumn of 1958, we felt we owed ourselves a working holiday in Australia. Frank Pope had booked us at the ABC Theatre in Blackpool for the 1959 summer season. We had eight months ahead of us and were determined to make the most of it.

JOAN To begin with I had quite a problem to sort out all by myself. Should I be a dutiful mum and stay with my children? Or should I be a dutiful wife and go with my husband? If the two children had been a little bit older we could have taken them with us, but it was really a terrible choice for me to have to make.

My first reaction was, Oh no, I am not going to leave them. Then, after about three weeks I thought, But I can't let Eric go all on his own and expect him to be happy about it.

The solution came from Eric's parents. Sadie said, 'Now look, we know exactly how you feel about this. We understand. But it's important you go for Eric's sake, and we will look after the children. In fact we'll enjoy looking after them because, really, we have all the time in the world.'

'But——'

'There'll be no buts. They'll be perfectly all right with us. I'll write to you every week about everything that happens, and I promise you faithfully that if anything goes wrong, or things don't work out, or the children fret, or we find it too much, I will phone you wherever you are, and you can catch the next plane back.'

So that was how we left it. Eric's parents were marvellous. Every week came a long bulletin with all the news. Not only were the children wonderfully looked after and ourselves spared all anxiety, but it proved a wonderful tonic for Eric's parents to have their grandchildren to look after. Gail was able to start going to the same junior school her father had attended in More-cambe twenty-seven years before, and school filled her life. Gary was only a baby in a high-chair and a total commitment, so much so that the plump little Nana we left them with was a much slimmer and fitter one we came back to.

Naturally, then came the heartbreak of taking the children away from their grandparents, but we did it gradually, in stages. Besides, we were near them in Blackpool when we returned so the blow was cushioned by regular reunions, and everything gently returned to normal in the end. Normal, that is, as far as family life was concerned.

ERIC Things were far from normal on other fronts. But we'll come to that. The object of the trip was to cram in as much as we could of the outside world.

The first American taxi we took from the airport to our hotel in New York was driven by a man who looked as though he had been a sparring partner for Joe Louis. He spoke with a larynx that sounded as though it could be used for grating nutmeg. He wore a tartan beret that was supported by two excrescences at the side of his head like bunches of dried figs—cauliflower ears, and he had an aura I came to associate with a type of taxi-driver BO mingled with stale cigar smoke. He charged us thirteen dollars and asked if we kids would like him to take us back to the airport because we didn't look like Italian immigrants about to take out citizenship papers.

'Sure,' I said, in my best American accent, 'we're taking the early plane to San Francisco on Monday morning. What's the flight time, Ernie?'

'Forget it,' said the taxi driver, whom I shall call Butch. 'I know the plane. I'll be at the hotel for you kids. Have a good time and don't run if a cop tells you to stop. Our cops carry guns.'

'We'll come quietly.'

Well, we were rubber-necking and didn't care who knew it. Ernie, for one, got his full money's worth. He saw every tourist sight, he travelled on buses, by the subway, he crossed the river by ferry, walked in Central Park, went up the Statue of Liberty, used the Pentagon lavatory. The cubicle lights came on.

He had made all the travel arrangements, and the hotel he picked was called the Sheraton McAlpine. On the reception desk was the notice 'we accept travellers' checks'.

We took the notice at its face value even if they did spell the operative word differently. We had travellers' cheques from a big banking combine with branches in every British town. Came Monday morning with all our ready cash in dollars spent. Joan and I left our bedroom and took the lift to the hall downstairs. It was about eight o'clock. Ernie was at the reception desk looking glum.

'You fix up,' I suggested. Ernie always enjoys administration and logistics and I let him have his fun.

'I can't,' he said. 'They won't take our travellers' cheques.'

I pointed to the notice.

'They've never heard of Barclays,' Ernie said.

'This can't be.'

'It's true,' said Ernie.

'Send for the manager,' I thundered.

'I am the manager,' said a voice behind the counter. He looked as though he had just come off a Mississippi showboat after playing Simon Legree. 'I'm not accepting *your* travellers' cheques. Try a bank.'

'But the banks don't open till nine. We have to get to the airport.'

'That's your problem.'

Ernie said, 'I've been round to the hotel next door. They would have accepted our travellers' cheques—if we had stayed with them.'

'What do we do?' I asked the manager.

'You can leave your baggage.'

I gave him a baleful look. 'Have you, by any chance, got a visitor's book?' I asked.

'No. Why?'

'Because I want to write something in it.'

'What's that?'

'Just this—"And we shall certainly tell our friends".'

Before he could answer we felt and smelt a draught. A nutmeg-grater voice said, 'Say, what's der trouble here?'

Ernie explained.

'Dat's no problem.' To the manager, 'How much?'

He was shown the bill—$50.85.

Butch produced a roll of crinkle, licked off 50 dollars, clicked off the rest in chink from a change dispenser he carried on his chest, and that was that.

'But how can we pay you back?' Ernie said.

'I trust you kids. Send it to me.'

'Thank you,' Ernie said. There was a catch in his voice.

As it happened, the banks at the airport were open by the time we got there and we were able to fix up with Butch and tip him handsomely besides.

San Francisco we loved. Dear Alma Cogan had given me a lovely cashmere pullover with the edges bound in soft leather. In San Francisco I put it on for the first time. We got to a crossroads. We were waiting for the lights to change when I took a drag on my cigarette just as a gust of wind swept round the corner and blew the burning tip off the cigarette. It lodged on the front of the pullover and burnt a dirty black hole in it. I could have wept.

Next stop Honolulu with a touch-down for fuel at a dot in the Pacific called Canton Island. Stepping off the plane was like entering a sauna bath. The sauna took an hour during which we drank coke and panted.

'Will all transit passengers on Flight Number So-and-So for Honolulu please board the plane through Exit Number Four. Have your boarding cards ready, please.'

We are back in the air-conditioned plane, strapped to our tourist-class seats. We are gathering speed when I look out of the window and flames with sparks like those you used to see belching from coal-driven engines are flying off into the darkness behind one of our engines. Hullo, is this for real? Maybe Ern and I can use the material in a show. Then, double-take, SOMETHING IS WRONG! The plane is shuddering. Eventually we stop.

Next, the voice of the Australian captain, 'Sorry ladies and gentlemen. A minor fault appears to have developed in one of our engines. No cause for alarm, but we shall have to return to the airport.'

It didn't help any when the panic was over and we had time to think about it.

Only one hazard remained, an electric storm. When it came it felt like riding a roller-coaster on square wheels. At last the aircraft landed safely at Sydney. We were told we were going into a lovely warm midsummer 'Down Under', having left behind the cold and wet of a winter in the Old Mother Country. Midsummer! We stepped out of the plane into a blast of freezing cold wind.

DOREEN The hotel in Sydney Ernie had chosen for us had swing saloon doors. You pushed and almost fell into a room with a long bar with long men without hips slugging back liquor. The place had a gold-rush air. I had read a book called *The Cry and the Covenant*, which was set in this part of Australia. In the story Condes fluid (potassium permanganate) was used as a disinfectant. But not in our Sydney hotel. In the bathroom was a notice which warned you, 'DO NOT USE CONDES FLUID IN THIS BATH'.

Breakfast came up—steak, chops, potatoes, ketchup and coffee. It was Sunday and nothing seemed to be happening except at the bar.

I said, 'When I was a baby my mother used to leave my pram outside the butcher's shop, and the butcher used to come and tickle my chin. When I was nine that butcher went to Australia. The name was Climpson.'

'He may be in the telephone book,' Ernie said.

We looked. Yes, there was a butcher named Climpson in the telephone book.

The phone was on the wall attached to one of those expanding hat rack affairs. I had to stand on a chair to reach it. I dialled the number. A voice said, 'Yes?'

'You wouldn't be the butcher who came from Peterborough, in Northamptonshire, England, a long time ago?'

'Well, yes, I am.'

'Well, I'm Doreen Blyth that was. I'm now married and I'm in Sydney with my husband and a couple of friends on holiday. We don't know a soul.'

'Where are you at the moment?'

I gave him the name of the hotel.

'Stay right there and I'll come round and pick you up.'

Which we did and we had a lovely day at their place talking about old times and the lives they had made for themselves in Australia.

We had to fly on to Melbourne—Eric and Ernie were booked for the summer season, but we all returned to Sydney for Christmas and went to the Climpsons' house for Christmas dinner. It was just like being in England, even to the cup of tea at tea-time which made us all very homesick.

JOAN For our part, Eric and I discovered several people we knew. We were in Woolworths in Melbourne one day when we met the son of a man named George Stead, who had sold Eric fish and chips at a corner shop in Morecambe. We met relatives of mine, descendants of my grandfather's brother who had emigrated to Australia years before. This grand-uncle was still alive and his children and even his grandchildren had grown-up families. They were strangers to me, naturally; and we had very little in common to talk about. Still it was nice meeting them We all had a great time together.

Then Eric discovered there was such a thing as a Lancashire Society in Melbourne; they even had a Morecambe section. They were all very hospitable and often on our free days off they organised trips for us to see places of interest for miles around.

The night the boys opened in Melbourne, the Lancashire Society were all in the stalls in evening dress. There was a knock on the dressing-room door. Eric opened it and a man said, 'I'm Brett Hall—or Bert Hall, as you knew me years ago. We went to school together. I'm now in real estate over here.'

DOREEN In Melbourne we found ourselves flats in houses overlooking the park. At our place the owner and his family lived on the upper floor and let the lower floor to show business people. Winifred Atwell was the star of the show with Eric and Ernie as second top. They were to be followed by another show starring Sabrina who had acquired TV fame virtually overnight assisted largely by a beautiful bosom. She was now touring in variety with two dogs known as her Two Beauties. In the house in which Ernie and I lived, Sabrina's arrival was a matter of almost daily discussion. The son of the house, a youth of about twenty and, I think, a little soft on top, was well clued up on her vital statistics.

'Will she wear a bra?' He wanted to know.

'Of course,' I said.

'That's a swizz. If she wears a bra in her act I'll ask for my money back.'

The obsession with Sabrina's bust continued. One morning, shortly before she was due to arrive, Ernie and I were in bed when I noticed some plaster falling on our bed. I looked up to see the point of a drill appear through the ceiling. The drill went back up the hole and an eye looked down on us.

Later the same morning, there was suddenly a face upside down outside our bedroom window. It wasn't Eric. It was the son, suspended by his ankles, trying out another vantage point in preparation for Sabrina.

ERNIE We spent three very pleasant months in Melbourne. We did well, helped a bit by the fact that we had followed a bad American show. We met a comic named Johnny Lockwood, whom we used to know in our early variety days. He had emigrated to Australia and was going over really big—using practically every gag and sketch he had ever heard in the Old Country including some of 'our' material! After that we weren't averse to using some whiskered and hoary stuff ourselves. It went down a treat.

From Melbourne, which models itself on Britain, we went to Sydney, which models itself on America. We had a flat over-looking Sydney's famous Bondai Beach. The swimming and the surfing, and some delightful beach house parties, made our two months in Sydney very pleasant.

There were several shark incidents which apparently are fairly regular. In one a child was actually taken from the edge of a swimming pool built on the shore. Shortly after that, two young sailors decided to race each other ashore from a ship anchored in the bay. They swam into a school of sharks. To people watch-ing from the ship it was rather like a burial at sea off Devil's Island.

Finally there was the incident in which Joan swam too far out, got caught by a current that would have taken her to New Zealand but for two bronzed Australian lifeguards. Eric was the only one in Sydney who did not know about it; in fact didn't know the story until it came out by accident thirteen years later!

We flew back via New Zealand and Fiji to Los Angeles. We had a look around Hollywood. Then we hit Las Vegas where Eric hardly saw the light of day as he played the machines, feeding in money and periodically running out and saying, 'I'm winning, I'm winning! Gimme another ten dollars,' and running in again while the rest of us were outside at the swimming pool, soaking up the sun, and waiting for Eric to come out again for another ten dollars.

As long as you didn't gamble you could have a good time in Vegas, at a low cost. The shows, the rooms and the food were all remarkable value. The desert air was clear and good, and the weather marvellous.

ERIC We made the girls work their passage in Vegas. We saw all the shows and they had to keep making notes of jokes and routines while Ernie and I did the drinking.

American food? I formed the impression then, and it hasn't changed, that American food looks great but it all tastes the same —like dentists' fingers. At a restaurant you would sit next to some ordinary American family. The waiter would come up and Father would ask, 'Elmer, you want a steak? Yes. Jane? Yes. Junior? Yes. Scott? Yes. And the same for Mom and me.'

The waiter would return with six large porterhouse steaks on enormous plates, with baked Idahos (potatoes as big as swedes) which they swamped with cream and chives. There'd be South Sea Island dressing and salad sauce and, on top of it all, more tomato ketchup than you'd ever see in the final massacre scene in a Japanese translation of *Hamlet*.

The family would start eating, father and mother smoking while they ate, their arms darting like octopus tentacles between the dishes and plates and the cigarettes on the ashtrays and the glass of beer or Bourbon, diverted every now and again to swat Elmer or Junior or Scott or Jane.

Then, before any of them were half way through, the meal would suddenly and unaccountably stop. The waiter would remove more than half of what he had originally served. Such waste of food shocked and continues to shock me.

Ernie had been warned before leaving England that if we exceeded our baggage allowance on a long air journey, it could cost a fortune. So we all started out with the very minimum, each of us well within our twenty kilos limit. The trouble was that inevitably you acquire things on a journey, so the only way round the problem was to *wear* the extra things you bought. We had enormous raincoats that went over this bulk of clothing, with four pockets in each raincoat bulging with knick-knacks. We may have looked like the bloated Michelin men when we checked in at the airport for the last leg of the journey, but we made it home to England without having to pay a single penny excess.

It was wonderful to be back but a shock was awaiting us when we contacted our agent, Frank Pope.

He said, 'You're lucky you're booked for this summer season

in Blackpool. Apart from that you've returned to an empty date-book. I can't get any work for you next winter. You've been away so long you're forgotten.'

12

ERNIE   We were not welcomed with open arms when we returned to the Central Pier, Blackpool, for the 1959 summer season. We were being paid £250 a week on a contract, signed the previous summer, and sharing the top of the bill with Jimmy James, but it was clear enough that we had lost ground with the public and the confidence of managements. The show didn't do good business.

But why? Was it that the people who visited Blackpool from all the towns and cities we would normally have played at during the previous autumn and spring and in pantomime for three months in mid-winter had actually missed us in the theatres and were unconsciously paying us off for neglecting them? Believe it or not, this was seriously suggested to us by way of an explanation by a well-known theatrical pundit.

No, we weren't the only people who had lost ground. What had happened during our absence was the beginning of a drastic change on the entertainment scene in Britain. Variety theatres had begun shutting their doors. To begin with, the Butterworth circuit of theatres, for which Frank Pope had the sole booking, had closed, leaving him with virtually nothing to offer us. This, coupled with very much stiffer competition for the fewer variety bookings that remained, meant that all he had to offer us were second- and third-grade theatres which wasn't good for Morecambe and Wise at that period.

Television was now the big entertainment medium of the future so Eric and I sat down and thrashed out the situation. We examined it and our position in it from every possible angle, and we realised we had to make a major decision.

First, we had to go into television, and secondly we had no option but to terminate our agency with Frank Pope. Our contract with him required that we gave six months' notice by registered letter, which we did.

It upset him, I know. We had become good friends over the years. Later, though other independent agents joined the big agencies, Frank carried on, trying to survive, till in the end he gave up theatrical agency altogether and joined Butterworths in a hotel venture which he helped to run with great panache. He missed the theatre, though. He still comes backstage to see us and talk about old times.

ERIC Meanwhile we had to find ourselves a new agent, so we put an advertisement in *The Stage* to the effect that Morecambe and Wise were now free, having ended their association with Frank Pope by mutual agreement and would welcome offers of agency. Before long most of the leading theatrical agents wrote to us. We had decided that the man we needed should be someone with good contacts in television.

I was sifting through the replies. 'Ernie,' I said, 'you know, there's one agent who hasn't written in.'

'Who's that?'

'Billy Marsh. He books for summer seasons all over the country, and for Bernard Delfont which means he can get us television.'

'Why do you think he hasn't replied to our ad? It was big enough.'

'Maybe, he hasn't seen it.'

Ernie pondered. Presently he said, 'You know, Eric, I think he's our man.'

'I agree.'

'What do you think we should do?'

'Let's write to him,' I said. 'Let's say we're free and would like him to take us on? That's all. You write the letter.'

Ernie loves writing business letters and he got down to it right away. The following day Billy phoned, and we went to see him. Slight and dapper, he smoked incessantly, flicking the ash over his left shoulder. We told him our story. That we were a standard act who had always had plenty of work, but could no longer get it.

'An excellent standard act,' Billy corrected. 'In fact, a standard act that should really be a top of the bill. But the only way to stardom these days is via television.'

'That's what we feel. We want to break into television and that's why we have come to you.'

'I'm sure I can get you TV,' Billy said, and with that he picked up one of his coloured telephones. He called a booker for ATV named Alec Fine. Billy said, 'I'm acting for Morecambe and Wise, who are available. I would like you to book them.'

'All right,' Alec said, and he gave Billy a booking right away for a spot in the ATV show, *Sunday Night at the Prince of Wales*.

Billy turned to us. 'That's it then, but remember television is not like touring in variety. Television gobbles up material and you can't use it again. It means providing instant personalised comedy in which your stage experience won't help you very much except perhaps with your timing. It's a totally different medium that few stage people really appreciate. But if you can keep coming up with good, fresh stuff, I can get you all the television you want.'

What he said made me feel a little weak at the knees, but we had to take the plunge.

'OK, it's a deal,' I said.

'The same goes for me,' Ernie said.

'We'll shake on that,' Billy said.

We shook on it with Billy and that's the only contract we have ever had with Billy Marsh to this day. Although he works for London Management, which is a very big agency, we have always paid his ten per cent fee for his services direct to him personally.

ERNIE Billy also booked us for our next summer season—at Weymouth on a variety bill with Anne Shelton. We played at the Alexandra Gardens, a rickety little theatre with a concert party atmosphere that has since been pulled down. They now have a theatre and ballroom called the Pavilion. Weymouth was a quiet, pleasant place to work in. We got less money—£175 a week, but we did well there, and Billy Marsh was as good as his word as far as TV was concerned. Before the summer season started we had had three spots on ATV's *Sunday Night at the Prince of Wales*. But that was only the start. Before the end of the year, *TV Times* noted that we were two of the most televised comedians without actually having a series of our own—we had logged up a further dozen appearances in *Val Parnell's Sunday Night at the London Palladium*, besides six in *Saturday Spectacular*, and four in *Star Time*.

In addition we were touring the country with the top American stars Bernard Delfont was importing. It was a great period.

ERIC How we started afresh on TV is interesting. We had to produce something different yet typical of us. We couldn't think of anything when one of us mentioned the judo routine. This was a bit of nonsense we had first tried out at the Central Pier in Morecambe in a TV show with Alma Cogan, Ken Platt and Semprini, the year before we went to Australia.

We had been approached by Eric Miller, a BBC–TV producer who now lives in Australia. He said, 'Do me a favour, boys. I have to produce a show from the Central Pier, Morecambe (which incidentally is a ballroom). It's an afternoon show. Can you appear in it?'

'OK,' we said.

He said, 'I don't know what is to follow you, but before your act there'll be a mock commando raid. We will have cameras outside the pier. When the tide comes in we'll be showing an "attack" on the pier by a dozen commandos with blackened faces. The studio audience will be in the ballroom. They'll be watching the attack on overhead TV sceens!'

'Fine. We'll think up something to suit the occasion.'

Came the show. The studio audience in the ballroom were OAPs. They heard shouts outside followed by bangs and machine-gun fire. On the TV screens they saw landing craft approaching, grappling irons being thrown, explosions, commandos leaping. But I doubt if anyone in the ballroom had the faintest idea of what it was all about.

From that the producer cut to the stage. This was our cue, and we went into our newly devised Judo routine.

'In view of renewed hostilities,' I said to Ernie by way of an opening, 'I think I'd better teach you the art of Japanese self-defence.'

'Japanese self-offence?'

'No, no, *please*! *That* can lead to blindness, stunted growth, loss of memory, excessive blinking and hair growth on the palms of your hands . . . Ah ha, you looked!'

'What about hara-kiri?'

'She's in the telephone book. Half rates after six o'clock.'

We developed it, going on to the Brown Belt, the Yellow Belt and the Black Belt.

Ernie Which belt have you got?

Eric The Purple Belt.

Ernie What's that for?

Eric To keep my trousers up.

Ernie What? I thought judoites didn't wear trousers.

Eric Enough of these exotic pleasures. Learn to fight. I am in a bar, having a quiet noggin. You come at me with a knife and I will show you how to get out of it. Go on, grab your weapon.

Ernie What?

Eric Imagine you've got a knife. Lunge at me.

Ernie lunged, I countered and was 'stabbed' under the right armpit.

Ernie Get out of that! (*Later it became a well-known catch phrase*).

Eric What went wrong?

Ernie I'm left-handed.

The audience just sat and stared at us as if we were out of our minds, so we immediately shelved the judo routine. Now, with no fresh ideas to hand, we decided to dig it up again for ATV, but with modifications.

We took the precaution this time of suggesting to the producer that he brought on two judo experts for a three-minute exhibition. We followed the experts with our routine, and it went down wonderfully. So well, in fact, that we used it three times after that on British TV, four times on American TV, and once in our first film, *The Intelligence Men*.

By now we had come to love doing television shows. They taught us a lot. Lesson No. 1—on TV in those days managements never took a chance with anything with the slightest hint of suggestiveness. The blue pencil is not a pencil that writes blue gags; it is a pencil once used by TV producers to remove mostly innocent gags with the zeal of Kremlin censors deleting passages from a Russian Nobel Prize-winning novel.

The Russians come to mind because of an uncensored gag we sprang on Val Parnell. It happened on the Sunday after Rudolf Nureyev had appeared the week before in tights which proved to several million viewers that, besides being a great dancer, he was a well-made lad.

In our spot we were doing a ballet routine when Ernie turned to me and said ad-lib, 'What about Rudolf Nureyev?'

I said, 'What about Rudolf Nureyev?'

He said, 'Didn't you see it last week?'

And I said, 'I'm sure everybody saw it last week.'

There was no immediate reaction. Then all of a sudden a laugh came from the audience like a wave, and it built and built so that we just had to go on with 'business' for about three minutes before continuing with the script. We were told off about it, but not seriously.

ERNIE Another lesson experience taught us was the importance of using time to the right advantage. We were stage-trained, the slaves of the stop-watch the stage-manager wore on a string around his neck. We were so well-disciplined about time that when Charles Henry, the producer of *Sunday Night at the London Palladium*, used to say, 'Lads, do six pen'orth of your best wheezers and get off,' we took him literally. We did six minutes and not a second more.

Only one thing worried us. We did notice that we weren't registering very well in the time allowed us. Six minutes isn't very much unless you work at break-neck speed, and if you do that you just don't allow the audience time to take in what you've said. What greenhorns we were.

I remember the night our eyes were opened. It was *Sunday Night at the London Palladium*. The act on the bill just before us over-ran his time. The producer who had been our stage director in *Strike a New Note* at the Prince of Wales when we were but glorified chorus boys, rushed up. 'Boys, I'm terribly sorry, but it can't be helped. You will have to cut your spot by two minutes.'

'Two minutes!'

'Yes, I'm afraid so.'

This was awful. Anyhow we went out and obliged. As you would expect, we made no impression on the audience at all.

'Thank you, boys. Much obliged. You're real troupers. You really helped me out of a jam,' Charles Henry told us.

It was nice of him to say that, but the public didn't know we were real troupers and that we had nobly helped out in a jam.

Next on the bill was a young man, all chin and self-confidence, ad-libbing like mad and manipulating everybody on the stage around him. He was down for seven or eight minutes, but he over-ran his time too, by nearly half as much again, or more. And he ended up paralysing the audience.

Eric and I had lost out on the deal all along the line. So the next time we were on the show, with an eight-minute spot, we kept it to eight minutes during rehearsals but during the show itself we let it run to fourteen. We ad-libbed to exploit jokes, we introduced extra material, and that night we also paralysed the audience.

As we came off, Charles Henry said, 'That was naughty. You over-ran. But, boys, you were really good. Great stuff. Congratulations.'

We were second on the bill that night, quite an achievement in itself in *Sunday Night at the London Palladium*. The next time we were booked for that show we topped the bill. It was one of the great high spots of our career as a double-act because we wowed the audience that night. We had learnt a major lesson in tactics.

ERIC There was a lot to be learned too from watching Bruce Forsyth. He is probably the only entertainer I know who is virtually the same person off the stage or screen as he is on. He

153

is all verve, vitality, always talking, looking for the joke, quick off the mark, razor-sharp but with perfect control, always chasing around and getting the most out of every possible situation. For some reason I could never get a word with him. I used to say, 'Stop, Bruce, speak to me!' But in the eleven or twelve years that have elapsed since those hectic days of *Sunday Night at the London Palladium*, that great TV show which made many stars, I still haven't managed to nail Bruce for a chat, *but hasn't he done well?*

In June 1961 the Lord Lieutenant of Devon, Lord Roborough, opened a new £200,000 theatre on the sea-front at Torquay—the Princes Theatre. Its first show was an extravaganza, presented by Bernard Delfont, with Joan Regan supported by Tommy Cooper; Edmund Hockridge, the Canadian singer; Morecambe and Wise; and a bill which included the juggler Ugo Garrido; the Munk Twins, singers and dancers; Patricia Starke, soubrette; the George Mitchell Four, singers; and a chorus known as The Lovelies.

At Torquay Eric and Ernie began the next phase in their lives. They were already very successful, but from here began their rise to super-stardom.

ERNIE   Torquay was a good place to be in. There was a nice show business crowd, including Jewel and Warriss at the Pavilion. We got together a lot at parties where we talked about precious little else besides television.

One day Billy Marsh rang me up. He said, 'Leslie Grade has been on the phone. He's quite impressed with the spots you boys have been doing on television, and he's offering you a live television series for ATV on Thursdays starting in October to run for thirteen weeks. Isn't that great? Now, you go and talk it over with Eric and let me know.'

Well, you must have gathered by this that Eric and I don't jump into anything without giving it a lot of thought. Occasional spots on *Sunday Night at the London Palladium* at £100 a time were one thing. It was wonderful publicity and you were usually riding the wave of a big American star. Providing the star wave for others to ride on was an entirely different matter, as we had found to our cost seven years before. Eric and I both felt the same way about it—very nervous.

Doreen and I had rented a flat in Torquay for the season. It happened to be immediately below the flat Ben Warriss had taken. Just opposite our flat lived an old couple. One night they woke up to find burglars in the room, and they got badly thumped about.

We knew that Ben Warriss used to leave Torquay every Saturday night after the show to spend the week-end in London. That Saturday night, at about two, we heard movements above in Ben's flat.

'I don't like the sound of that,' I said to Doreen. 'I'm going to have a look.'

On the way I grabbed a poker and, finding Ben's front door ajar, I dashed in and was about to brain Ben with the poker when I recognised him in the nick of time. He had turned back because of fog. Then Doreen appeared, wondering what was going on. Result, a few noggins over which I explained our problem of the TV series.

Ben said, 'For a TV series it's vital you have the right ideas, in other words the right script, and that it gets better and better as the weeks go on. Thirteen weeks is a long time. We were lucky with our writers—Hills and Green, who also did a brilliant series for Dave King. We were also lucky in our producer, Colin Clews. He's the best comedy producer in television.'

I said, 'Ben, do you reckon that if we got Hills and Green and Colin Clews we would be successful?'

He said, 'Yes, I'm sure you would.'

Next day I told Eric about our conversation with Ben Warriss.

'He's absolutely right,' Eric said. 'Phone Billy Marsh and tell him we'll do it if we can get Hills and Green and Colin Clews. Money doesn't enter into it. We've got to have the right people.'

Back came the reply, through Billy Marsh, that we couldn't have the people we wanted, but we could have anybody else.

We said no, it had to be them.

Would we or wouldn't we do it? We'd be utter fools to refuse. We stuck to our guns. Deadlock. The whole thing was off.

Then—we are not sure of this but we suspect—the Grade Organisation got stuck for a comedy half-hour on Thursday nights, it was coming up to October and the result was that Dick Hills and Sid Green came down to Torquay with a record by Johnny Mercer called *Two of a Kind*. It became the theme song and in fact the sub-title of *The Morecambe and Wise Show*.

ERIC Actually the title *Two of a Kind* was I think more applicable to Sid Green and Dick Hills. They were both ex-schoolmasters. Both had been to the same school in London—Haberdashers' Aske's. Both had become school captains, played rugby (Union naturally) for Kent, and had written pantomimes for the school amateur dramatic society.

One day Sid met Dick and told him he was going to write some funny scripts for Dave King, and Dick said, 'Yes, let's.'

'I don't remember ever asking him to help, but by that time he had a wife and two kids so I couldn't bring myself to refuse,' Sid said.

That was the beginning of their collaboration. By the time we met them they had written material for Harry Secombe, Bruce Forsyth, Sid James, Lance Percival, Roy Castle, Charlie Drake, Tony Newley, Dave King and Jewel and Warriss.

They were once asked a few years later how long it took them to do a script for Morecambe and Wise. Dick replied, 'We can devise a Morecambe and Wise job as we pass one another in opposite directions on a tube escalator.'

I believe it. At the height of our most successful period with them, Dick would arrive at rehearsals with a single sheet of paper with, as a title, 'Our Ideas for the Week'. For which, incidentally, they were paid more than we were, and we were getting £400 a week for the series.

Sid would come late. Something always happened at home to delay him. We used to call it his 'touch of the domestics'. We—the four of us—produced the rest of the script by collectively ad-libbing around it while a girl took the gags down, the draft was rushed out, polished and finally rehearsed.

We were content although their first Morecambe and Wise offering hadn't been the happiest. I remember a sketch in which Ernie and I were supposed to be spies. I pointed out there were so many people in the sketch I couldn't find Ernie, but I was over-ruled. The experts knew what was good for us, or so they thought. As we had predicted we did not register. The show went out from the Wood Green Empire—it had been converted into a TV studio—and that night the audience were lukewarm to say the least.

The following week our dogmatic writers came up with an even more thickly populated sketch. The jokes were there. We had some very funny lines, but again we were sure it was *wrong* for us.

Then, to our good fortune, came a crisis in the television industry. Equity, the actors' union, went out on strike and with them most of the people in our show.

Dismay.

'You're done for,' said Sid.

'Not at all,' we said, 'we belong to VAF (Variety Artists' Federation).'

'But what about sketches? You can't get VAF members, jugglers and acrobats and the like, to play acting parts, and you don't want other comics.'

'God forbid,' we said.

We thought about it, discussed it between ourselves, then said, 'We can play all the different parts ourselves—the old woman, the *femme fatale*, the lecherous old man, the Nazi general and the others with quick changes of costume. It will give the sketch a completely new dimension on TV, besides keeping it personal to ourselves.'

Which was what we did, and it made all the difference. The strike lasted twelve weeks, long enough for us to establish a successful format for ourselves from which we have never deviated. As far as we are concerned, in our shows the fewer people the better.

Meanwhile the scripts from Hills and Green got progressively better. We gained confidence which in turn generated ideas. Dick Hills would arrive at the studio at about ten, Sid Green, shall we say, in due course. It was remarkable how well we jelled. There were arguments, plenty of them, but oddly enough ideas stemmed even from differences of opinion. In the middle of a verbal scrum somebody would mention something and the rumpus would abate, as though a referee had blown a whistle. The thought would have clicked simultaneously with everybody. Then, slowly at first, then with mounting excitement we'd build on to it.

ERNIE Yes, many great ideas sprang out of arguments. One that comes to mind was a delightful bit of nonsense. Eric comes on with a yo-yo. He's a yo-yo addict. He can't leave it alone.

> 'I'm hooked,' he says. 'I've got to have my yo-yo all the time.'
> 'I can cure you of that,' I tell him.
> 'You can't. I'm a hopeless case.'
> 'Easy,' I reply and cut the string.

We had a succession of top guest stars, and every week a different trad band, led by people like Acker Bilk, Kenny Ball, Terry Lightfoot. We had a regular spot called *Home From the Wars* built around my stopping Eric as a returning soldier from kissing a pretty girl in a different situation, say as a soldier back after six years abroad and waiting to go straight upstairs with his wife.

We had Eric being promised every week that he could do as his finishing number his greatest dramatic acting role—his Gettysburg address as Abraham Lincoln, or his Fagan, or his Jekyll and Hyde, and putting on his costume and make-up, and my stopping him at the last moment with the words, 'But we've run out of time.'

And last of all, as we'd go off the set by a door, there'd be the final surprise pay-off—the door would open on to a brick wall; or as we'd open it custard pies would hit us in the face; or as on one occasion, it was to an express train hurtling towards us and we shut the door just in time.

Great stuff which brings back nostalgic memories, and with them the memory of our first accolade in show business during that winter of 1961—a place on the bill of a Royal Command Variety Performance.

13

ERIC I remember the occasion well. We were doing a summer season at the Palladium in 1964 with Eve Boswell, Pearl Carr, Teddy Johnston and, at the top of the bill, Bruce Forsyth. We were chatting in Bruce's dressing-room, the Number One which, at the Palladium, is like an underground bunker—there's no window. Any moment Adolf and Eva might walk in.

Bruce was talking about a fantastic season he had had at Blackpool in 1960. 'Unfortunately,' he said, 'I was ill for the first week with mumps and they filled in for me with a load of rubbish.'

'I remember the time,' I said. 'And I remember the load of rubbish who filled in for you. This load of rubbish took turns. There was Tommy Cooper, a big load of rubbish! Albert Modley, another load of rubbish! And Morecambe and Wise, a third load of rubbish!'

Poor Bruce. He had really put his foot in it. Ernie and I weren't doing at all well in the show but the incident put us in such good humour, and that, combined with some happy ad-libbing, enabled us to lift the act out of its doldrums. In fact we paralysed the audience that night, and who should be sitting in the stalls but one of the most powerful men in American TV—Ed Sullivan.

Ed liked us too, and when he liked an act big things happened for it. They happened for us. It was perhaps our strangest show business adventure.

We were booked for three spots on Ed Sullivan's weekly show with its estimated audience of fifty-three million. The New York taxi driver who picked us up at the airport was most impressed.

'Say, you folks English?' he asked by way of openers, after we had given him the name of our hotel.

'Sure,' I said, 'Yorks and Lancs. The girls are Eskimoes.'

'Get away.'

'We've just arrived.'

'You're show business. Shakespeare?'

'Try again.'

'Trapeze act?'

'We have a swing in the garden.'

'After a crack like that you can't be comics.'

'Yes we are. Double-act, Morecambe and Wise. Tell your friends to look at *The Ed Sullivan Show*.'

We were doing sixty. He looked back at us forgetting the road.

'You guys on *The Ed Sullivan Show*! Gee, you're made because Ed's big, very big. When he's in Town he lives in two suites—not one, two suites—in the Delmonico Hotel.'

'Please, the road. . . .'

'Gee! Two suites in the Delmonico!'

Ed must have been seventy. He looked like a sour edition of Humphrey Bogart which is the point at which a face can curdle milk. His show was nothing more than a simple stringing together of a number of variety acts. Of it he was undoubtedly the star yet he never appeared to DO very much, and even what he did he usually got wrong.

He began by introducing us as Morrow, Camby and Wise, then looked around for the invisible third man. On top of that he described us as a European act.

'British,' we corrected. So the next time we walked on the stage it was to the strains of *Rule Britannia*.

We had a song, *Boom Oo Yata Ta Ta*, that we had rehearsed with him. His part in the song was just to sing 'Boom'. Even that he couldn't remember.

Still he was so successful he could do virtually what he liked in the running of his show. He booked the biggest and most expensive acts in the world, and some of the American ones commanded astronomical fees. That meant nothing if he wasn't satisfied. We saw him fire and pay off top people, and that happened whenever he didn't think they went over well enough in an afternoon run-through of a show before a studio audience. This audience was very carefully picked and was representative of his total TV audience, not only in its elements but even in their estimated proportions. You would see him watching perhaps a bunch of nuns, noting their response to jokes and situations. It was a totally professional and American approach to entertainment. And we approved and tried to learn from him. It is all very well for an individual producer to have a flair for knowing what the public wants. But producers get older every day while audiences, as Caesar noted of the crowds lining the streets, always remain the same age. Fashions, preferences, joke reactions, accents, even language, keep changing all the time. You must have some uncommitted and impartial means of keeping with it.

Ed Sullivan was very particular about the running order of his show. I remember in one show in which we appeared with Tommy Cooper, Tommy closed the show in the afternoon run-through. In Britain, to close a show is the big thing. It's the star's place on a bill. Tommy was pleased. He had been very good and got some terrific applause. But just before transmission time that evening, Ed Sullivan reversed the order and Tommy was told he was going on first.

Suddenly the world collapsed for Tommy Cooper. 'He can't do this to me! Terrible! I'm ruined! I'll ring Miff [Miff Ferrie his agent]. God, this is terrible! Give me a drink! I can't take it!'

'Tommy,' I explained, 'you've been put on first *because* you did so well. It's the way things are here. There are so many TV channels to choose from, Ed Sullivan puts his best act on first so that the viewers, when they see it, will not switch to something else.'

'You're only saying that. I don't believe you. I can't face anybody, even the lavatory attendant. He won't even offer me a towel now. Before it was, "Howdy, Mr Cooper. Would you prefer a blue towel or striped? Most folks like the blue." Now he's walking away.'

'Your tip was too small.'

Eventually we succeeded in calming Tommy down, but he remained far from happy.

ERNIE After the first show, we had a week to wait for the second. As we had return air tickets, it didn't cost us very much more to fly down to Miami, in Florida. We stayed at the Fontainbleau. It was about the same price as our New York hotel, which Ed Sullivan was paying for, so we weren't very much out of pocket. This time the four of us went together which was nice. On another trip on which we combined two Ed Sullivan shows, Doreen and I went to Barbados, and Eric and Joan went to Jamaica, which made a change and in its own way was nice too.

Anyhow, in Miami together, we all led each other astray. The first question was, 'Where are we going tonight?'

Sammy Davis Jr was on at the Fontainbleau. What could be better? For twelve dollars each you ate and could see the floor show.

'That's where we're going,' chorused the girls. 'What value!'

They were the bosses, but they hadn't reckoned that in addition you could only buy drink by the bottle, at ten dollars for gin, which the girls asked for, and ten dollars for whisky, which Eric and I wanted.

'What's it to be, Scotch or Bourbon?' the waiter said.

'Bourbon,' said Eric in his Butch Cassidy voice, 'and don't bother with a corkscrew. I'll bite off the neck.'

'It's not a Bourbon chicken,' said the waiter, and walked away.

Eric looked at me. 'I know that accent—Manchester.' Eric thinks he's an expert on accents.

'OK,' I said, 'but be more precise. Salford?'

Eric was frowning darkly. 'Did he say, "It's not a *Bourbon* chicken", or did he say, "It's not a Bourbon, *chicken*"?'

'What's the difference?'

'Infinite.'

Anyhow, up came the gin and up came the Bourbon.

'Where do you come from?' Eric demanded.

'Sir?' said the waiter with disdain, and turned away.

To cut the story short, while the girls were content to have perhaps two modest gins out of their bottle, Eric and I were hanged if we would let any of ours go back to the establishment.

'We'll deny them that perk,' Eric said.

'I agree,' said I. So we drained our bottle of 90 per cent proof Bourbon.

When Sammy Davis Jr left the stage we got up to go. The waiter barred our way.

'Now what?' Eric demanded. 'We've paid the bill.'

'You have forgotten something.'

'Oh,' said Eric. 'I know what he means. Largesse. Ernie throw him a dollar.'

I offered a dollar, but quickly increased it to five dollars. The unveiled threat in the man's stance acquired a special menace. I upped the offer to ten dollars. The man took it.

'And I thought you were from Manchester,' said Eric. 'No Mancunian would act like that.'

'Sir, I am from Salermo in Sicily,' he said and walked away.

That wasn't our only misfortune. Outside in the fresh air we are carefully negotiating the front steps of the hotel when who should thump me on the back, rattling all my teeth, but—and my eyes began to focus—Ed Sullivan.

'Oh boy, oh boy! Fancy seeing you guys here!'

'It's a small world,' I stammered.

'Not small enough. Great to see you. What are you doing here?'

'Came down for a few days.'

'Wonderful. What are you doing tomorrow? Like to come to the horse races?'

'Love nothing more.'

'Fine. Great,' said Ed. He couldn't get over Eric's real name, Bartholomew.

'Mr Bartholomew——'

'Sir?'

'That name's got class. Remember Freddie Bartholomew? He always stood up when a lady came into the room. Bartholomew and Wisdom, you've got a good act.'

'It's Morecambe and Wise,' said Eric.

'Who's Morecambe?'

'I am.'

'See that white car?' said Ed.

163

'It's a Rolls,' I said.

'Got class, eh?'

'Sure.'

'It's mine,' Ed said. 'It will call for you tomorrow.'

It did, but not to take us to the races. That was off. Anyhow, the Rolls, with us in it, crunched up a mile of gravelled drive to a beautiful millionaire Hawaii Five-O type house with a swimming pool, a brook, a lake with a motorboat, and an outside bar with a coloured barman playing a cocktail shaker like a maraccas.

Eric was still green from the Bourbon debauch of the day before.

'Try the meat balls, Mr Bartholomew, they're the speciality of the house,' Ed said.

I saw a pile of greasy brown lumps in a fog of garlic-smelling steam that would have killed any insect unlucky enough to fly into the cloud. I looked at Eric. His 'poorly look' had returned but in Technicolor-green, the dark rings under his eyes muddying into a slime-green.

'Eric,' I advised, 'I'm sure you will love them. Mr *Sullivan* has *recommended* them.'

Ed was watching Eric cobra-like. 'Take one in your fingers Mr Barthomomew—it's fingers here . . . Yes, you got the idea . . . Now dip it in the chili sauce, Mr Barthomomew . . .'

I tried to distract Ed's attention, but Ed was pressing home his point. He was a student of human reactions and Eric was under study.

'Fine, Mr Bartholomew. Now roll it about in the chili sauce. It will do your liver good. Now pop it into your mouth and chew.'

Eric dared not demur. We were getting four thousand dollars a show plus expenses. In went the speciality of the house. I saw Eric take a bite and his eyes begin to pop.

'Good,' said Ed, satisfied. 'I'm glad you could take it. Most of you British are too soft in the mouth.' He had lost interest in the torture and turned his attention to Joan and Doreen. Eric meanwhile was siphoning soda into a glass and transferring it to his mouth.

'Now, what can I offer you ladies?' Ed was pulling out all the stops.

'I'll have a Pimms,' said Joan.

'Me too,' said Doreen.

'A what?'

'Leave it to me, sar,' said the man with the maraccas. 'Dem drinks have class. I can fix 'em.'

'You do that, real good, mind.'

'Yus sar. Two Pimms Specials coming up.'

Ed looked around. 'Say, where's Mr Bartholomew?'

'He won't be long,' said Joan. 'He's saying how d'you do to the plumber.'

'Who? Oh, very good! That boy's got class! The taste buds—delicate.'

ERIC   You'll note that there is no reference to fish and chips. What Ern seems to forget is that the class image which I brought to the act upped the money we got from Ed Sullivan to seven thousand five hundred dollars a time for four minutes plus first-class air travel, not to mention a large bottle of Scotch and a large bottle of Old Grandad's Bourbon in our respective suites in our hotel in New York on the day we arrived. One of these rooms was the scene of a strange orgy.

That morning we had visitors—Hills and Green, with Roy Castle, who was doing a spot in the Gary Moore show, and Roy's pianist, Jeff Saunders. We asked them what they'd like. Dick Hills wanted hot soup and crusty bread rolls, but Joan said no, adding in her curiously illogical way, 'The beds aren't even made.' And, incidentally, has never been allowed to live it down. I suggested a drink, early though it was. The motion was carried, and in no time at all, American hotel room service being what it is, we had a trolley being wheeled into the room clinking melodiously with bottles and glasses.

Whisky, gin and vodka had been asked for. To save the waiter a journey I had ordered two of everything. The alcohol had come in jigger-sized bottles of the sort you get served with on a plane. With them were bottles of soda, tonic and American dry ginger. Drinks were poured, hands reached for them.

Sid and Dick were too very amiable characters. Dick Hills we used to call Father Christmas because of his Pickwickian red cheeks and love of good cheer. He had asked for vodka and tonic. It was known that he did not have much of a head for drink and soon he was merry. Within the hour he was getting really maudlin and sentimental. In fact he was tight.

Eventually lunch was suggested. As the bottles and glasses were being collected and stacked on the trolley, somebody noticed that the two jiggers of vodka hadn't been touched. The person dispensing the drinks had forgotten all about adding vodka to Dick's tonic. He had got drunk on plain, undiluted tonic. So we gave him the vodka to sober up.

ERNIE The Americans were very kind to us. Once, when we were booked to play in Toronto, in Canada, the entire Ed Sullivan unit flew over to support us. On another occasion Ed took us out to a restaurant and bought us a dinner, a great honour for a visiting act.

One day Eric and I were walking down Broadway when we saw our names outside the theatre from which the show was transmitted. We were completely knocked out. Our names in lights on Broadway! We rushed back to the hotel to get the wives to feast their eyes. Then we went backstage in the theatre to thank Ed Sullivan and his son-in-law, Bob Precht, who handled their advertising and publicity.

'Thank you very much, you've made our day,' we said.

'How come?'

'You've actually put our names out there in lights. We're thrilled beyond words.'

Bob Precht seemed embarrassed, so we went out to have another look. Our illuminated names had disappeared from the front of the theatre porch. Anyhow, later, out of kindness, they were put back again for a while.

We did about four Ed Sullivan shows a year for four years. Frankly, in the end, it got too much for us. Besides which we didn't really enjoy being in New York. Joan stopped going because she couldn't stand the central heating, particularly in midwinter. There were times when we would step out of a hotel heated to 85°F into the street at 0°F or 32°F below freezing.

I remember once remarking to a man spiking up leaves in Central Park that it was nice to be out in the fresh air.

'The trouble about fresh air is that you can't control the temperature,' he replied. He was dead serious.

Another thing Eric hates flying. I used to try to anaesthetise him before take-off with a good slug of whisky. But you'd see him gripping the arms of his seat like a condemned man in an electric chair, and he'd stay like that until we landed in New York. Twice when Doreen and I went on ahead to stay with friends in New York, and Eric followed, his plane overshot the runway on landing. Believe me he was in a fair old state when he got to us waiting to meet him at the airport.

Doreen and I had our unpleasant flying experiences too. On one flight to New York our plane was full of American soldiers returning from Vietnam, all drunk and quite uncontrollable. It got to the point at which Doreen was airsick and she had never been airsick in her life. All this was bad for our performance. We also found that we were beginning not to score too well there, despite all the kindness and consideration shown to us. Eric used to call it our five minutes of agony.

By then we had seen all the sights, and seen and heard a lot more besides. Things you've seen only in *Bonny and Clyde* films come as a shock in real life—hoodlums with their hands up on car roofs being frisked by the police; people being pulled out of gutters and thrown into black marias; a dead body at a street corner; shots coming from a hotel room followed by police sirens; empty taxis refusing to stop for you outside a cinema because it was late in a doubtful neighbourhood.

We got to the stage where we would arrive on a Sunday morning, do the show that night, collect our cheque, pay our income tax the moment the tax office opened at nine in the morning, and be on the next flight home. Later, by arrangement with the tax people, whereby we gave them a cheque for our income tax in advance, we were able to catch the midnight plane home on the Sunday night. On one of these return flights, the co-pilot of the plane did a double-take as he passed by where we were sitting. He stepped back and stared.

'I don't believe it,' he said. 'Tonight I saw two fellows the spitting image of you two on *The Ed Sullivan Show*. The chances of two pairs of doubles occurring must be billions to one. Excuse me, but I must tell the Captain to come and have a look, otherwise nobody will ever believe me.'

'All right, we own up. We were the two you saw on television, but don't tell the police. We're making a quick get-away,' said Eric.

That night, with a tail wind, we broke the existing Atlantic record for a passenger plane.

ERIC: Our final Ed Sullivan show was in May 1968, a special show put on as an eightieth birthday salute to Irving Berlin on CBS-TV. Not only was the regular Ed Sullivan hour extended to ninety minutes for the occasion but the show was introduced by the President of the United States, Lyndon B. Johnson, speaking from White House. It was quite touching, the President assuring the eighty-year-old immigrant from Russia, who became America's greatest songwriter of the twentieth century, that the debt he thought he could never repay the United States 'has now been settled in full'.

Ed Sullivan had lined up an enormous bill of American stars, so it was an honour for us to be invited to appear on it. Unfortunately we were given so little time it was impossible to put ourselves across.

This was the review in New York's *Daily News Record*: 'Like most Ed Sullivan shows it lacked style, precision and glamor, but unlike most Ed Sullivan shows it was entertaining. Ed mispronounced several names, technicians walked accidentally across the screen and although we were saved from elephants, jugglers and sadistic puppets, there was one curiously out-of-place vaudeville team called Morecambe and Wise which should remain England's problem, not ours.'

Which brings us to the difference between the British and American sense of humour. Can our brand of comedy travel the Atlantic even when we are doing the same sort of material in the same language? At one time our style, our approach, even our accents, were American. We began as a vaudeville cross-talk act at a time when every second British comic was a mini-Hope.

Over the years we have evolved away from that model. Our style has become a very carefully rehearsed ad-lib, if you like, which keeps looking for the ridiculous in situations. Several critics have very flatteringly observed that we have made inane material funny; we hope we will be forgiven if we gently point out here that this is the general intention. We begin by looking for inane material; the reverse rather of the Tommy Cooper technique of finding comedy in bungling really good material with magic thrown in and turning it upside down. Tommy too has been misunderstood, and not only on paper. In one Midland town the audience became hostile. This is a perfectly true story. 'Look at that fellow, he can't do a trick,' they were saying. 'This shows how little he thinks of us, the swine.' At every show their resentment got worse. Tommy found himself being followed back to his digs by a gang bent on beating him up. Tommy's a big fellow, so I doubt if any of them had the guts to get close enough although they called him all they could think of. It wasn't very nice. It was a week of torture for Tommy.

Any act or material that is good will travel, but you need time and exposure to get through to the massive television audiences in America before you can persuade them to laugh at your particular sort of nonsense. The feeling we have at the moment is that the Americans, who worship at the altar of professionalism, still seem to think that at heart we are really amateurs.

Far from it. Every line, every pause, every move in our act is thoroughly rehearsed. Perhaps now and again, if a spot is going well, one of us may slip in an ad-lib, but we are so much on each other's wave-lengths after nearly thirty-five years of close association that this usually sparks off a spontaneous new wisecrack in return or one of several thousand gag-responses which we have exploited together countless times before.

Our initial problem at the start of our career was putting ourselves across, in getting audiences to share with us in our intimate sense of fun. There were times when we were received without a titter, a not uncommon experience for comics. But we found as we developed that we were beginning to catch on as audiences began to 'tune in'. Mind you, it wasn't all one-way. We were searching for what they wanted and dying to give it to them, so that when eventually we found our feet on TV in 1961 we clicked. Then we got better and better with each successive series.

The art, we found, was in making it look easy; indeed this proved to be the most difficult part. The essence of our act is what we call the mutual trigger. Neither of us is the comic nor the other the feed, though we may appear to some people to slot automatically into these two separate roles. For ourselves, our plan, has been towards becoming two characters, each imagining he is the masterful type while the other is the foil but nevertheless has to be kept happy by being allowed to believe he has the upper hand. It's a case of where one doesn't know the other doesn't know who's the boss. Or is that too involved? Well, then, put it roughly this way. One is an idiot but the other is the bigger idiot though he tries harder not to show it. One, oozing self-confidence, comes on with some debonair idea. The other, self-opinionated and supposedly slick and worldly-wise, goes along with the idea in order not to deflate his friend whose morale needs a prop, and they finish by sending up the idea which was nonsense anyway.

Our situations are timeless. They are intended as a droll commentary on the human scene, satirising it by ridiculous oversimplification. This sort of mockery is self-perpetuating. Our act remains unaffected by events and we never bring in politics or make cracks about politicians.

The catch-phrases have come accidentally or by exploiting weaknesses of our stage characters—Ernie's vanity, for one, in 'You can't see the join' in the gags about his wig. The truth is that I am the one who admits he is going a little thin on top while Ernie thinks he has a beautiful head of hair. Does that make sense? If it doesn't, don't kid yourself that I'm going to let out any of the little fellow's personal secrets because I've had a privileged view of him in his underpants. That wouldn't be fair, but this is a perfectly true story. A friend of ours was on holiday when he overheard a man in a hotel bar saying he *knew* for sure Ernie wore a wig. 'I happen to be his hairdresser,' he added, and that was the end of the argument.

Well, the strange thing is that Ernie hasn't got a hairdresser. He doesn't need one.

What we would dearly like is to be able to put ourselves across in America. All the great American comics—Laurel and Hardy, Abbott and Costello, Hope, Kaye, Skelton—were launched around the world from Hollywood. But it was always more or less a one-way traffic because British comics were never able to 'travel' far in the generally inept, low-budget films made in

British studios, and that dismal story can be traced back to the 1930s. We too have suffered—from three unsatisfactory films that came out of Pinewood. A friend of ours saw the third, *The Magnificent Two* in a flea-pit of a cinema in Amman, Jordan, with Arabic sub-titles. There were eleven people in the audience despite a commando raid with sten guns by a platoon of girls in bikinis which were so brief that one girl lost her bra during one of the takes and didn't feel the drop—in temperature.

We are not blaming anybody for these mistakes. They were ours. We were too busy chasing the Wooslem Bird of success. Our sense of values had become so distorted that we had only one reply to any proposition, 'How long and how much?' The result was that we didn't take, or rather we neglected to seek, the best advice, and we lost out on many important things. We hope we have learned our lesson.

14

Eʀɪᴄ We earn our living telling funny stories. Few of them are real but the one we are going to tell you now is the absolute truth, we promise you. You can always recognise a pro who has been used to working on the stage because the last thing he does just before he goes on is to check his flies.

We used to have a routine in pantomime in which Ernie was the officer in command of a squad of soldiers, usually chorus boys, with myself standing right at the end of the line.

Ernie 'Squad, from the left, number.'
    (*The squad would start doing the rumba.*)
Ernie 'I said "number", not "rumba". Now let's try again. From the left, number.'
    (*The squad would begin: 'One', 'Two', 'Three', 'Four', 'Five' and so on, but when my turn came I would say, 'One'.*)
Ernie: 'No, no, NO. You are not one!' (*pointing to the first man*), 'He's one.'
Then all the others in chorus: 'But he's *one* too!'

On the day this incident happened one of the soldiers had his flies undone. There used to be a joke we could sometimes pull on a pro on the stage. You would whisper, 'Psst, don't look but your flies are open.'

One's immediate reaction in a situation like that is to panic and

172

look down. The test of a true pro is that he doesn't panic. He will contrive to turn his back to the audience, check and if necessary unobtrusively make good the omission.

Now, the chorus boy in question had heard about the joke—no, he wasn't going to be caught out. Then he began to have doubts—people had kept on about it. But, not being an experienced pro, he did the one thing you shouldn't. He looked down. Immediately the audience's attention was drawn to the undone flies, and Ernie with great presence of mind shouted, 'Arrest that man. You, about turn. You two on either side of him, by the left, frog-march. Left right, left right, left right left.'

He turned to the audience, 'Like the two fellows sitting on deckchairs in the Sahara. One said to the other, "It's nice out here." '

I went forward. 'You can't tell that story *here*!'

By then the audience were in stitches, but we were ticked off about it by Bernard Delfont—he thought we had set it up. We managed to talk our way out of that one, but why have we brought up the story here? The answer is because there's a moral to it, and it's this. No matter how secure you think you are, you have a weak point somewhere. You can come unstuck. We know. It happened to us, and here are the facts behind this frightening epic.

Let's go back to 1963, that wonderfully successful year for Morecambe and Wise. Packed houses at the North Pier, Blackpool, for twenty weeks that summer. Our third TV series reached Number Two in the TAM top twenty TV ratings, second in popularity only to *Coronation Street*. We topped bills in *Sunday Night at the London Palladium*. We were voted Britain's top TV Light Entertainment Personalities of the year by the Guild of TV Producers and Directors. That Christmas the pantomime in which we appeared at the Bristol Hippodrome broke all previous box office records for the theatre. As for the money we were making, Ernie, who still has the same notes Jack Hylton paid him, couldn't close the suitcase of fivers he keeps under an old wig for a quick getaway.

Since we had first teamed up in a railway carriage between Coventry and Birmingham, in 1939, we had pursued only one aim—success. But success with certain reservations. Ernie, in his steady, cautious way had always held that it was preferable not to top bills.

'Second tops are better,' he would say. 'Let's just stick to being a good, reliable act. It's safer. You can go on and on as a second top till you're ready to qualify for the old age pension.'

Nobody else had ever made an ambition of second top; it isn't normal in human nature not to reach for and dream of stardom. But we weren't *normal* comics. We were cunning comics. So cunning in fact that at one time it scared us even to share a top. People who topped bills had a notoriously short life. The top was an extremely difficult position to sustain, and managements, ever sensitive to the slightest drop in box office temperature, are the most fickle wooers ever. Once you have topped bills, it's hard, not just to step down on a bill but even to get work. So we had plumped for regular work. In such matters I am always guided by Ernie who gets a kick out of being wise.

'We're in show *business*,' he used to say. 'It's OK being an artist, but it's the businessmen who make the money. They don't get their names in lights, but they turn on and they turn off the lights. We have to keep on our toes, we have to worry about applause: all they do is add up the balance sheets, and if the profit isn't good they get somebody else. We're like footballers—great, as long as they're scoring goals. It's the managements, the faceless ones with the thick necks and fat cigars, who come off best. We unfortunately were seduced as kids by the glamour, the glitter, the applause. OK, we're artists. But let's keep our feet on the ground.'

So we had played safe. But success, wonderful, bewildering success, had overtaken us in spite of ourselves. The year 1964 bounded in leaving us breathless, intoxicated. Whatever we touched turned to gold, or so people said. Money was pouring in, but wasn't that what we had been striving for all these years? Who could complain? Only it seemed the trouble with big money, making big money, is that it becomes a terrible habit. You can't refuse a good offer—after the tough early times you've been through, you hate turning anything down. Indeed your conditioned reflexes make it impossible. You have become like Pavlov's dogs, except that, instead of salivating when the bell rings, your hand goes involuntarily into the signing twitch.

174

Behind it all too is the thought that you mustn't upset the powers that be, that you need managements as much as they need you, that other people are to be considered. Now that you're in demand you have obligations and responsibilities.

So it began, what Fred Allen called the Treadmill to Oblivion. For us it was the plodding round of show after show after show. Before each the pleasurable anticipation, then the fears, the returning insecurity—will they reject us? The rituals of make-up and superstition. The familiar dressing-room smells, the pinpricks of discomfort, the butterflies in the stomach, the tributes, the deferences, the knock on the door. That bladder again though you know it will be only a few drops, a nuisance to be shaken off. The ascent into the wings. The girls on the brightly lit stage garish in close-up, damp with sweat as they crowd past you. The darkened audience—what are they like tonight? The drum roll, then suddenly you're on and no longer yourself but an addict in an adrenalin fix that takes you through an hour and a quarter of a sort of unendurable pleasure indefinitely prolonged to a climax of final applause and a detumescence that leaves you sweating and shaking, clear-headed about every detail of the performance, but curiously numb to all else. People are talking. Drinks being offered. Bustle. Sounds. Faces. People, people. Doors shutting so loud they hurt. Then you're limp, sitting in a chair, peeling off your wet clothes, slugging back a drink, dragging on a cigarette . . .

This is success. This is what you have stalked and captured, this triumph of successful suffering, this spasm of creativity but not the creativity of something finite like a building or a statue, but a creativity so much more lasting because you have fixed in time a moment of satisfaction for a polyglot entity called an audience, participated in it, and centred their attention upon yourself, which is something on which you are hooked.

Have you watched a pair of oxen, hitched to a persian wheel, stamping round and round on a path their hooves have beaten hard to the strange grinding and creaking of the age-old machinery and the chain of buckets scooping up water from the well. In a sense we were like a pair of draught animals except that they at least know where they are going and seem content, whereas our plodding was in the wake of a ridiculous illusion that ultimately everything would be wonderful for us and we would find some nirvana in super-stardom and Croesian wealth.

These were lures, like the papers reporting we were the highest paid double-act in showbusiness. Yes, we did start earning big money but we also started having to pay big tax. By the time we did reach the super-star bracket as earners, all but all, the tax loopholes had been plugged.

The funny thing was that we didn't seem to mind the treadmill at the time. We had been so brain-washed along the road by stories of top acts being unable to work that we never complained. To us as entertainers the idea of workers demanding less hours of work and more hours of leisure for the money they earned was totally incomprehensible. The entertainer never wants less working time. The man with the ten-minute spot longs to be the man who comes on last with a seventy-five-minute act. Now that we were in this enviable position we worked compulsively as the pantomime treadmill became a TV series treadmill. That was followed by a treadmill of touring in variety that took us into a treadmill of summer seasons, then back to more variety and Ed Sullivan shows and, at the end of that, back full circle with the start of yet another Christmas pantomime.

You wouldn't think another treadmill was feasible but a contract was signed with Rank to make *The Intelligence Men*, adding yet another variation to the continuous round of all work and no play. When we moved into our new home in Harpenden, where we still live, during the first year I spent a total of less than twenty days in it. It got to the stage where coming home was like living in a film in which things happen magically. One day a wilderness of weeds in which a wooden shed was scarcely visible had become a beautiful garden with a lawn and rose beds. Another time there was a translucent blue swimming pool where before there had been rubble. Extensions appeared. Colour schemes changed.

What we used to look forward to in normal years were the two weeks' rehearsal before a pantomime began. On 22 December 1964 we were still at Pinewood filming *The Intelligence Men* although it had been anounced several weeks before that we were opening in *The Sleeping Beauty* at the Palace Theatre, Manchester, on Boxing

Day. Tom Arnold, who was presenting this show, had already taken over £100,000 at the box office.

We got to Manchester late on 23 December, a Wednesday. We were playing the King and Jester, parts that luckily we knew because we had played them in the same pantomime the Christmas before. On Thursday, Christmas Eve, we had our first rehearsal for a two and a quarter hour show in which the part of the Prince was actually played by a man, Edmund Hockridge.

Came the opening on Boxing Day. Twenty minutes before curtain-up, disaster. One of Ernie's front teeth, that had been pegged and capped, became involved with a biscuit and went down into his stomach with it. (I was told he never did find that tooth, but a day later he hobbled in on bent knees. 'I've been bitten,' he said.)

Anyhow, during panic stations with everyone rushing round in ever-decreasing circles, a man in the show called Bertie Hare quietly went out to a chemists' shop and came back with something called gutta-percha. It looked and felt like chewing gum. Ernie stuck a bit on the stump. It covered the gap until he was able to get to a dentist next day.

During the run of the pantomime, we were awarded Silver Hearts by the Variety Club of Great Britain as show business personalities of the year. We were told we would have to come down to London to a luncheon to accept the awards, but obviously couldn't because on the day of the lunch we had to be in Manchester appearing in a matinee. To our surprise the management announced that they had cancelled the matinee so that we could fly down to London to collect our Silver Hearts. But immediately after the lunch we had to catch the next plane back to Manchester for the evening show. It was really big of them because money had to be refunded, though I do know that most of that matinee audience exchanged their tickets for alternative bookings.

A pantomime with a run of twelve to sixteen weeks is hard work, especially if it is successful when you have to do two shows a day for a good ten weeks. During that period you can have no social life, and unless you take a stroll around your hotel after breakfast, which you have in your hotel bedroom at about eleven, you won't sniff very much fresh air or see many rays of sunshine.

In the old days in pantomime it was possible for us to get a nap between shows. It was a rare luxury now for there were all sorts of fresh demands on our time. It was heaven when the matinees ended, but then came the requests for personal appearances, from opening supermarkets or departmental stores to presenting prizes to carnival queens or saying a few words at a village fête. There'd be PRO stunts like modelling pullovers or being photographed with a collection of beer mats, sandwiched between the shooting of a TV ad or an interview with the press.

Press interviews were particularly tiring for you were expected to sparkle in order to provide material for your so called image off-screen. There'd be telephones ringing all the time. There'd be conferences with your dogmatic script writers who would come to discuss ideas for the next TV series or rather outline to us the areas of likely future argument. Our collaboration with Hills and Green was fruitful but not the fun it had been with Frank Roscoe in *Variety Fanfare*.

ERNIE I think I was better adapted by nature to cope with the treadmill. Eric is a worrier and a perfectionist. He puts a great deal into a performance. I do too but it takes more out of him emotionally than it does out of me. You need your Sunday off if only just to put your feet up which was all both of us really wanted to do. But if you also have to work on a Sunday from lunch time until eleven at night, rehearsing and topping the bill in a *Sunday Night at the London Palladium*, sooner or later you're going to become unstuck.

This happened to us on Sunday 21 March 1965. I remember Eric had been complaining about being tired. There was nothing to be done about it, but as the *Daily Mirror* reported, our act floundered badly.

'Many of their jokes misfired. Several were just unfunny, and a sketch in which a girl was supposed to be doing a striptease behind a screen ended without a proper payoff.'

Actually, worse than that had happened. We were wearing radio microphones around our necks. Radio microphones are fine. They enable you to move about without having to trail a length of wire behind you as if you're doing the hoovering. But you do have to be careful of the switch which has to be turned on

178

while you are in the wings, waiting to go on the stage. Forgetting this, Eric remarked, 'Jesus, I hope they're a better audience than we had last time.'

It went right round the hall, which meant we were welcomed with only very desultory applause. In the act we then hit into snag after snag. Finally, with a last stab in that night's orgy of professional hara-kiri, Eric made another remark as we left the stage, again forgetting the radio microphone.

He said, 'That must be the worst bloody act we've ever done.' Back came the answer from the audience, 'YES!'

It wasn't easily lived down. We were in pantomime at the time. In the show Eric's opening words as we walked on the stage were, 'Have we got a show for you tonight, have we?' To which we invariably got a roar of welcoming response.

The night after the gaff, a voice promptly shouted, 'I hope it's a sight better than the one you did last night!'

In show business you can't afford a flop at any time, least of all when you're at the top. So you can imagine how we felt when *The Intelligence Men* proved a critical disaster:

'An unspeakable British farce in which two stage and television comedians, Morecambe and Wise, are fed through the Norman Wisdom sausage machine (by the team responsible for the last Norman Wisdom film) and come out looking as though they could not make a hyena laugh. What a shame, and what a waste of time for all concerned.' *The Times*

'. . . Norman Wisdom please come back.'

Evening Standard

'*The Intelligence Men* reminded me of Bud Abbott and Lou Costello at their worst.' *The Sun*

'In *The Intelligence Men* we have to watch the ruination of those two excellent comics Morecambe and Wise, in an embarrassingly unfunny spy skit.' *Sunday Express*

'. . . a chaos of flat gags . . .' *The Observer*

'It has a few laughs . . . but is a good deal less funny than you'd think from two such masters of lunacy.' *The People*

179

I could go on in this vein but it's depressing and it still doesn't do Eric's nerves any good. His problem is that he is naturally incident-prone but under stress he becomes accident-prone. At the time when the reviews of our film were striking us like bolts from the thunder god, Eric decided to go out with a friend of his to a stretch of river near Wimbourne in Hampshire, for a day's fishing. Now Eric is one of those people who should never be allowed to handle a rod. He has been known to cast a line and catch himself. He can't swim, yet he never fails to fall into the water—his father, when they go fishing together, never lets him out of his sight.

On this occasion Eric was on the bank of the river, spinning for salmon, when he saw a mound of grass about three feet from the bank. Thinking that if he could get on it he would be in exactly the right spot to cast down-stream, he took a flying leap and landed on the green patch. It was not grass—his glasses had lied. It was green slime and he sank up to his neck in a stench that followed him around for days.

A few film reviews later—I believe it was on the same stretch of river—the cap flew off his vacuum flask and his clothes were drenched with hot coffee.

And again, a few more film reviews after that, as a consolation he took his wife to the theatre. I think I have mentioned Eric's punctuality. With him punctuality is not just a fetish it's a terror from which he can start pouring sweat. When we toured in variety he was known to be at the stage-door even before the stage-door keeper.

When he goes to a function, he allows for every possible eventuality including punctures and breakdowns. He had been seen waiting with Joan in a car, both in evening dress, a full hour before a dance was due to begin at which we have been guests of honour and expected, in the normal way, to arrive a bit late. Eric is a director of Luton Town Football Club, has been for four years. He has his own parking spot and a salute as he goes through the gates. He just has to walk to his seat and sit down. On a Saturday the match starts at three. Eric has never been later than 1.50 pm—because he never has had a puncture, a breakdown, accident or encountered heavy traffic on the twenty-minute journey.

To return to Eric's and Joan's evening out. The idea was to get to the theatre a good half-hour before curtain-up, have a pleasant cocktail at the bar, and then stroll down to take their places in the stalls. Unfortunately for them it was pouring with rain. Joan gets out of the car and waits in the foyer in her mink coat while Eric goes off to find a garage to park the car.

Half an hour later the foyer is full of people, but there's no sign of the man in her life. Another half an hour passes, the foyer is now empty and Joan is still waiting and by now very worried. At last two men arrive.

'Mrs Morecambe?'

'Yes.'

'We're terribly sorry, but your husband has broken down in Leicester Square.'

She goes with them and there, conveniently opposite the AA headquarters, is her poor Eric, drenched to the skin with his smart suit ruined.

Their car is towed away. It is too late to go to the theatre, and they can't face going to a restaurant. There is nothing else for it but to take a train back home. But the train journey is awful. The compartment they choose has been slashed by vandals, there's vomit all over the floor, and to make matters worse there's a man in it eating egg and tomato sandwiches.

So ended their sad evening, but they weren't allowed to forget it. Next day came the galling truth, when Eric's garage owner went personally to collect his stricken car, that there was absolutely nothing wrong with it. That expensive and temperamental creature purred with responding affection the moment the garage owner's caressing hand touched its erogenous starter.

ERIC Ref, stop him. He's taken that line from his plays.

ERNIE I haven't finished the episode. No, that's not all. There's the last, the final straw—a bill for £25 from a man whose car had been grazed by Eric's as he was trying to find the parking place.

Don't get me wrong. I don't mind carrying Eric on my back, as I have done all these years, but please appreciate the difference between us.

ERIC *Vive la différence!* That's French. There was this little French girl in school——

Whistle

ERNIE Thank you, Referee. What I want to explain is that he and I are curious opposites. I am, I think, what I would call a cautious optimist, while Eric, by that token, is an incautious pessimist. I will say a theatre is half-full; to him it's half-empty. Either way it frets him if anything is short of perfect or wholly right in his life or work, and when you boil it down with him the two are synonymous.

When Eric is strung-up or annoyed he lets off steam, but never at work or with show business colleagues. He and I are noted in the profession for being the easiest people in the world to work with and for; this is a boast and we are proud of it. We have been disciplined by working with people. We are used to things not always clicking the way you plan. I can discuss a mistake gently. Eric will almost invariably say nothing. On rare occasions, over a drink after the show, he might remark that it could perhaps have gone better if such and such had been done. Eric will say nothing more—until he and Joan are on their way home alone in their car. Then, quite casually, he will ask 'How do you think it went?'

Now all that Eric wants from Joan is praise, because underneath it all he is really working only for her. The ideal answer she can give to this question is, 'Great'.

But Joan is no fool and Eric knows it. He knows too that she knows she's got to be strictly honest. She can't wriggle out of it. She's got to say something like, 'Fine, but . . .' and that's when Eric blows up. Joan is Eric's safety valve and it's an important function because once he has got his irritation off his chest he is released from it.

Before a big show, he tends to start letting off steam at home, and Gail and Gary, who recognise the signs, discreetly avoid the storm centre or as they put it in weather forecasts 'areas of high pressure'. Great kids.

I, for some reason, possess an immunity. This isn't just a trumpery publicity story, it's the literal truth. We have never fallen out, and one reason for this, I suppose, is that I'm so loveable. The other is possibly that Eric has fundamentally such a major problem on his mind he has never got around to falling out with his better 50 per cent.

At the core of his nature Eric is a very introverted person. Very shy, hating the embarrassment of being singled out in a crowd, of being stared at, of being approached. Yet the job he chose or, as he would rather have us believe, was thrust upon him, is by definition extrovert. It demands that he should make an exhibition of himself. Here is the conflict in a nutshell.

He would give most of what he possesses to be able to shed the mask of Eric Morecambe and slip into a kind of amorphous anonymity in which he can be just an ordinary guy taken at his face value, preferably as a stodgy type but friendly and cuddly, in a circle of respectable, reliable salt-of-the-earth types in the five to ten thousand a year income group.

Unfortunately for him he cannot merge into the crowd. His face is too well-known, and this means that he has to sparkle when he would rather relax. At a big function you can understand how things are with people continually coming up for autographs, and being sincere in what they say. You want to be nice in return, but sometimes you would give anything for the odd five minutes when you can just let yourself go and droop without being observed. You can't, and in these situations I think it is easier for me than for Eric to coast along. I am more equable; Eric is different. He is working—performing, on the alert and ad-libbing with quick-fire gags from the moment he steps outside his front door, whether he is at a parish fête, at a warm-up before a studio audience or in a restaurant at a corner table with Joan and his audience only three waiters.

Scores of invitations come from people who don't know you from Adam, who will say that all they would like is for you to come to their do and enjoy yourself when in fact this is the last thing possible with everybody present watching to see if Morecambe and Wise are really as funny off the box as they are on.

In fact Eric can stand up to this pressure of being the focal point of attention, of giving of himself all the time, better than most people. He can go on for hours when others about him are wilting. But Joan will tell you that the moment he gets back home he begins stripping on his way up the stairs. She follows him, after taking the dogs out, and will pick up his jacket, trousers and shirt where he has shed them on the floor on his way to bed, and she will find him usually in a deep sleep.

ERIC One of the pressures of the showbiz treadmill is its greatest honour—the Royal Variety Performance with its inevitable jockeying for dressing-rooms, for billing and, most of all, for selection for the line-up of acts to be presented to the Queen Mother who is patroness of the show and for years has had to sit through a marathon of entertainment every November. Not only does the show itself play havoc with the nerves, and here the Americans seem to suffer the most, but the prospect of meeting members of the Royal Family can be frightening to say the least. You might think that entertainers, trained in the art of talking, would never be stuck for a word when it comes to chatting up the royals. Far from it. You are terrified and when the time comes you tend to dry up.

One male comedian was so overcome he actually curtsied instead of bowing. But the classic story of a line-up concerns Peter Sellers. On being presented to the Queen Mother, Peter bowed correctly. Her Majesty must read *The Stage* because she usually knows just where you are currently booked. She might say, 'I see you did well at The Talk of The Town. Congratulations.' That night she wasn't sure about Peter.

'What are you doing at the moment, Mr Sellers?' she asked.

All Peter could say was, 'Standing here, Your Majesty.'

It is altogether different at Windsor Castle where you are invited to help put on a show at the Staff Ball and the whole occasion is informal and quite delightful. The Queen usually comes and chats to you. One year, I remember, after she had spent some time talking with us, she suggested we went in and had supper. A beautiful meal was laid out in a small room for those who had taken part in the show. We had scarcely sat down when Her Majesty came back. Peter Brough, who had organised the entertainment, immediately went up to her.

Peter told us later that she said, 'Oh, I see that Eric and Ernie and their wives have started supper. I don't want to interrupt them. I just wanted to say how sorry Margaret was she couldn't be here tonight as she is such a fan of theirs.'

The next time we performed at the Windsor Staff Ball, Prince Charles said, 'I hope you don't mind, but I used some of your material in a sketch we did in college.'

When we look back we find that somehow the big things that have happened in our lives can be grouped into compartments, usually geographical. During the four years that Joan and I shared a home with her people at the Torrington Arms at North Finchley, we kept our expenses down to a very modest scale and saved hard. Our ambition was to buy a nice house. We spent quite a time looking around for a suitable place, and while we were looking the prices kept going up and up. One place we saw would have been ideal for us. It was opposite the park at Friern Barnet, with parquet flooring throughout, but the price was £4,000. No, we certainly weren't going to pay that so we decided to wait.

'Prices are bound to come down,' I said.

Today that house would fetch £30,000. When Ernie said I was not a financial genius he was right.

Anyhow our financial position kept improving and we were able to have a house built near Harpenden. Gail was eight and Gary six and they went to local schools. It was a happy house. Only good things happened in the five years we lived there. Then our financial position became better and we bought a bigger place in the same area. The new house had become run down but it was in a very nice position. It required a great deal being done to it, anyhow this was a challenge and we had great plans. For some reason, and this spell lasted nearly three years, things began to go wrong the moment we set foot in this house.

First, Joan had to have an operation. Then my mother arrived. Sadie was being shown around the place when she stepped into a gap in the floor where an electrician had lifted the boards in the kitchen and hadn't replaced them before going off to his lunch. She had to be rushed to hospital. Several stitches were put in her leg.

Then, one peaceful Sunday—I had that day returned from an Ed Sullivan show in New York—we heard a car arrive outside. Gail, my beautiful daughter, had been brought home by some people. She had been out riding when the horse became uncontrollable, she had jumped off, and it had kicked her in the face.

Her nose was broken, her jaw fractured, and her flawless, lovely teeth stove in so that some were embedded in the back of her throat. The horseshoe had missed her eye by a fraction. You can imagine her state, and ours.

We rang our doctor—he lived nearby. He rang a dentist, and both were waiting at Mount Vernon Hospital when the ambulance arrived with Gail in it. There was an immediate operation, and we were waiting when she came out of the theatre unconscious, her face already swollen up and turning black and blue. It was heartbreak.

Anyhow, I am glad to say the surgeon did a wonderful job. Her nose and jaw have healed perfectly. She lost two front teeth but the gap has been filled with two false teeth on a permanent bridgework. The others were saved.

ERNIE   By January 1966 we were into our fifth successful TV comedy series for ITV, and we were going from success to success in variety and pantomime. But there had been another two films, *That Riviera Touch* and *The Magnificent Two*, both, like the first, written by Hills and Green, and panned even more mercilessly by the critics. The critics were right—and we are not blaming Hills and Green. They had been called upon to produce a script based on a formula decided by a production committee. This was a hotch-potch of what had been found successful for other funny men in films for the past forty years. On top of that it all had to be done within a penny-pinching budget.

While we were making *The Magnificent Two*, a volcano was being built for a James Bond film, *You Only Live Twice*. The volcano cost £250,000, which was more than the entire budget for our film. All we got out of our films was a fee. In addition, we were promised we would become millionaires out of the profits. I am not saying the films didn't make money—I am told they did. But we didn't receive any of it.

The *Sunday Telegraph* said this of *The Magnificent Two*: 'What it offers is what *Film Fun* used to offer its faithful child readers.'

To which I would like to add that in *Buster*, the children's comic (there are grown-ups' comics too), there was a strip called *Morecambe and Wise*. This strip was full of our fictitious adventures and the funny things that happened to us. I was looking through some back numbers of *Buster*, and it struck me it was a pity our film producers didn't look among those strips for film stories for us. Some are really funny.

Meanwhile in our own business, the one we understood, things were going very well. Our summer show in Great Yarmouth broke the theatre's previous record. We did a successful LP called *An Evening With Ernie Wise at Eric Morecambe's Place*. Lew Grade sold £2 million's worth of colour TV shows to North America including a 13-part Morecambe and Wise series with Millicent Martin. These shows were smash hits, especially in Canada, but we didn't think our deal with ITV was altogether satisfactory for us. The upshot was that we did not renew our contract with Lew Grade. Instead we signed a contract with the BBC who could give us colour on BBC-2.

By 3 August 1968, recordings of the BBC colour show had started. Then bookings began to pour in and it came to the point that overlaps were inevitable and all sorts of subtle pressures were being put on us in the hustle for our services. We did something we wouldn't have dreamed possible even a few months before. We turned down an offer to star in the West End, a show business peak that had previously eluded us. There was better business to be done touring the Northern clubs, as Prince Philip had once suggested to us.

Meanwhile Joan had been getting increasingly worried about Eric. He was smoking between sixty and a hundred cigarettes a day and living on his nerves. None of those who worked with him, including myself, quite appreciated the pressures he was under. Eric on the surface has a very bland manner and an even blander sense of humour. At the same time he's a hypochondriac with never any qualms about letting you know of every twinge he suffers.

As far as I was aware he was in as good health as myself, though when I think back on it now, I realise we were crazy to accept the sheer volume of engagements that were beginning to swamp us.

We were working a very nice club outside Darwen, in Lancashire, where Eric stayed at a hotel called The Last Drop. Jane Russell was there at the time, and Eric, like our landlord's son in

187

Melbourne, used to salivate at the thought of watching her undress through the window, waiting for the last drop!

We were due to open for two weeks at the Batley Variety Club. We were rehearsing two spots to take over to a club in New York, a big new deal for us. We were planning more colour TV for America. We were talking about a Christmas show which we were to do in Glasgow for eight weeks.

That was the position in Darwen when a second telegram came from Bernard Delfont asking us to appear in the Royal Variety Show. He wanted us for no less than four spots. We had already turned him down on the grounds that we just couldn't cope. This second telegram was to beg us for his sake to help him out, that it would do us the world of good in the profession and that he personally would never forget it. What can you say to such a plea? We wire back yes.

We opened in Batley on 3 November 1968, a Sunday. We knew Jimmy Corrigan, the club's creator. Jimmy came of a Leeds fairground family. Through sheer hard work he had built up a Bingo empire in the area, then gambled all he possessed in a venture that had become an entertainment phenomenon, and others in the North were quick to copy. There were fifty thousand members of his Batley Variety Club. They were attracted there by good, plain inexpensive food, cheap drink at a large semi-circular bar at the back of the vast auditorium and top entertainers whom he attracted by paying the highest fees in Britain.

We were doing an hour and a quarter, starting at midnight. On the Thursday night Eric complained that he wasn't feeling very well. After the show he said, 'Ernie, if you don't mind I'll go straight back to my hotel. Could you cope with the autograph books?'

Usually a pile of autograph books would be brought up after the show. We might spend half an hour signing them.

'OK,' I said. 'You carry on.'

'See you tomorrow, then. Good-night.'

I glanced up as he walked out. I thought he looked a bit drawn. I turned to Doreen who was in the dressing-room. 'I hope he'll be all right.'

'Don't worry,' she said, 'it's just his "poorly" look!' It was a

The (not so very) *Intelligence Men*

Manny and Eric, Pipemen of the Year

'Eric, who's that little fellow with you?'

George and Sadie's Golden Wedding at Morecambe in February
1971

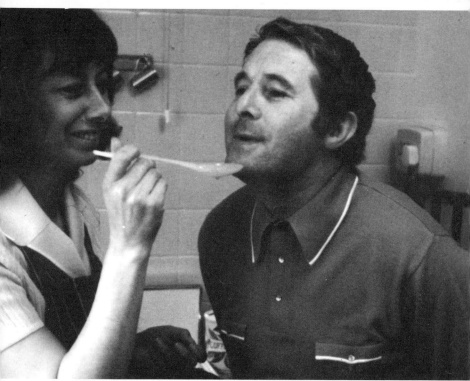

You won't believe it, he's never been in the Morecambe pool
Still in the galley thirty years later, and you pay for it
Note the draw of the bow and the cut of the trousers

SFTA Award night at the Grosvenor. Johnny and Wynn Ammonds (*foreground*) and (*anticlockwise*) John Antrobus, ourselves, Eddie and Diedre Braben and Graham Braben

The payoff—Barbara Murray and Ann Hamilton

In the line-up to be presented to Her Majesty the Queen after a Royal Television Gala Performance

Defusing the wallet on location at Peterborough

The Grapes of Glenda

joke between the four of us and we laughed. We had been too busy to realise how tighter and tighter our own gyrations had become. Eric was already on his way to a deadly rendezvous. It was the night of the Wooslem Bird.

PART THREE

Afters

15

ERIC   There is nothing very scenic about Batley; you need to be born there to see the beauty in its lovely Coronation Streets. Batley is about eight miles from Leeds. Jimmy Corrigan's Variety Club is just a hundred yards away from a spot where a pub once stood in which his great-grandfather was murdered in a drunken brawl. Jimmy pointed to the spot when he was showing me around. In front of the club two brand new Rolls-Royces were parked, one Jimmy's, the other his wife's.

They lived in a beautiful house he had built on a hill a short distance from his theatre club. The house is L-shaped, with a patio and paved garden walks under rustic arches trailing rambler roses, and a drawing room with a chandelier made from an old coach wheel and an enormous polar bear rug before the stone fireplace. The head was red-eyed, panting. Then it seemed to snarl at me and at that moment I felt the first twinge.

It was in the arm, rather like a tennis elbow or a bit of rheumatism. Whenever I pressed that arm, the right, in the funny bone region I would get a shooting pain; incidentally, I still do.

Now who would guess that this was an early warning of an invitation to an oxygen tent. I am the hypochondriac, remember, the fellow who is even supposed to complain that he may have to complain of some complaint he may only suspect he may get. With a reputation like that you tend to want to be stoical, to suffer in silence, just to show the scoffers you are made of sterner stuff.

So I took no notice of the arm. I worked on the Monday and Tuesday. I didn't feel great—I felt rather like I do now! Wednesday? The same. But Thursday, awful—from the morning when the pain in the arm started to get really bad to right through our 75-minute spot which included a couple of tap-dance routines and several acrobatic falls.

By that time platoons of waitresses had cleared the tables of the remains of Jimmy's dinner menu—chicken, steak, scampi, ham and, of course, chips. There were just drinks now, drinks with the bar waitresses moving about like wraiths, fumbling expertly with the change and gesturing their thanks. Meanwhile the audience was being wonderful. I remember a great chorus of bassoon-like laughter from the region of the bar. This lovely laughter worked like a prop every time I thought I was going to stagger.

Then it was all over, and Ernie has told you how I opted out of the autograph books.

I had a Jensen Interceptor at the time. I was staying at a hotel in Selby, twenty-nine miles away, the way I went, through Leeds. As I was driving, the pain started to get worse, and I thought, This is the sheer funk of a born hypochondriac. I was sweating. That confirmed it was funk. But what was I afraid of? Never for a moment did I suspect there was anything the matter with my heart.

Severe pains started shooting across my chest and back. With automatic gears and power steering the effort of driving was not too much, yet by the time I was getting into Leeds I began to feel I had better find a hospital. I looked for road signs but saw none, and at a quarter to two in the morning there weren't many signs of life either.

There was a man on the pavement, waiting to cross the street. I stopped. Almost in a whisper, I said, 'Please, could you direct me to the nearest hospital?'

He looked at me cautiously. 'Oh, ah, let me see. . . . Oh yes, go up this street here—it's all one-way, which makes it a bit awkward. Then take the third right—no take the second right. Then carry on and take your third, no your fourth left . . . Then you'd better ask again because it becomes complicated.'

I said, 'Look, I don't feel very well. Could you possibly drive me there?'

'Well,' he said, scratching his ear, 'I'm in the Territorials, I've only driven a tank. Never anything like this.'

I said, 'There's nothing to it. It drives itself.'

'OK, I'll have a bash. Ee, you do look poorly.'

'That's always been my trouble.'

After a little fiddling, we shot forward. 'Ee, this is not a bit like tank,' said Walter Butterworth. I got his name later when it came to the autograph.

Soon we were climbing a rise. We stopped under a porch. Walter went up some steps. The door was closed so he knocked on a big, curtained french window. I saw the curtains pulled back by a silhouetted figure and the window was opened.

'Who's that?'

'There's a fellow here. He's taken ill.'

'Oh. Well, we don't accept emergencies here. You want the Infirmary.'

At the Leeds Royal Infirmary, instead of taking me to the Casualty entrance, Walter left me in the car on the street at the bottom of the hill on which the hospital stands. They do it the hard way in the Territorials.

'I'll go for a wheelchair,' he said and hurried off through the hospital gates.

At the front entrance he was stopped by a janitor. 'Who are you and what do you want?'

'I want a wheelchair. I've got Eric Morecambe in a car. He's not feeling very well.'

'Oh, yes? Ha ha ha!'

'Please, it's serious.'

'Well, you'd better go round to Casualty, oughtn't you?' So Walter went to look for Casualty. Meanwhile I wasn't improving so in the end I got out of the car and walked up the slope to the hospital. The Leeds Royal Infirmary is a huge, spacious building with a magnificent front staircase. It is beautifully run, it has a fine reputation and they look after you wonderfully—once you get in!

I too went to the wrong entrance, was directed to Casualty

which I recognised by the queue of black eyes, cut heads, bleeding noses and generally roughed-up looking men and women waiting for attention.

I staggered towards a man in a blue uniform and peaked cap at a desk. Walter was with him. I was about to give my real name Bartholomew, but stopped myself my brain ice-cold clear. Something told me to pull out all the stops.

I said, 'My name is Morecambe of Morecambe and Wise. I don't feel at all well.'

The blue uniform turned to Walter. 'You were right. It is him.'

'I told you it was him,' said Walter.

'By golly, you don't look good,' said the uniform.

'I don't *feel* so good,' I said.

'Do you want to be admitted to the hospital?'

'Yes.'

'Do you have a letter from your doctor?'

'No.'

'Do you want to admit yourself?'

'Yes.'

'All right, that's in order. Now, name?'

'Morecambe.'

'Same as place at seaside?'

'Yes.'

'Fore name?'

'Eric.'

'Address?'

At the end of the questionnaire, I said, 'Could I lie down?'

'All right. Lie on that trolley. I'll try to find somebody for you.'

On the trolley I now began to worry about the Jensen. In Leeds, the police have a habit of towing away cars left in the street.

'How do you feel?' He was about twenty and straight from the cast of *Doctor at Large*. 'A bit of chest pain? Where is it?'

I told him.

'Hm.' To the orderly. 'Pull down his pants.'

I was turned over, down came my pants, in went a needle.

'You'll feel better in a few minutes.'

'Oh, doctor,' I said.

'Yes?'

'I left my Jensen on the road. The police . . .'

'A Jensen, eh?'

'Yes.'

'All right, I'll move it for you.'

I gave him the keys. Presently he returned. 'I've moved your Jensen into the car park, and locked it. It will be all right there.' With that he placed the car keys on my chest and left.

I still had no idea it was a heart attack. There were no palpitations of the sort that make your shirt look as though you're trying to hide a lively squirrel inside it. But I was speeding along a corridor ahead of a pretty young nurse full of chat about taking me to X-ray where they would see all my dark secrets.

In the X-ray room, somebody said, 'Just sit up.' (Apparently something you don't do to a heart case!) A big square plate was brought up to my chest, the X-ray shot taken.

'Could I have a private room?' I said.

'OK.'

By now, from the cross-talk, the ice-cold brain figured it was a heart attack. I thought of Peter Sellers and his heart attack during one of his honeymoons, and how he was brought back from death three times by heart massage. Nothing as dramatic as that was happening to me. Just a second injection that had eased the pain and was lulling me gently to sleep. Somebody touched my trolley.

'It's Walter Butterworth, the fellow who drove you to hospital.'

I opened my eyes and thanked Walter for all he had done.

'That's all right, Mr Morecambe,' he said. 'Look, my mates at work will never believe me. Do me a favour. Before you go— (his very words, I swear)—*before you go*, could you sign this for me.'

He put a piece of paper on my chest and a stub of pencil in my hand, and very shakily I signed 'Eric Morecambe', convinced it was my last autograph.

My next memory of that night is of waking up in a strange sort of haze and for a moment the thought crossed my mind that I had just died and was passing out of this world into the after-life.

Everything was deathly quiet except for a funny sound that went *beep-bo, beep-bo, beep-bo*. Gradually I realised I was not on my way to heaven but was in a plastic oxygen tent. The sound was coming from a kind of television screen on which a dot of light kept hopping up and down as it wandered across the screen till it went off one side and started up again on the other.

Fascinated, I watched its performance for a minute or two. To me in that state it seemed quite an original routine—why hadn't we thought of it before? Then, as I took in more of my surroundings, I realised I was not alone. I had company. An extremely pretty nurse was sitting under a shaded light reading a paperback with a lurid cover. I became aware too that wires were emanating from me, glued to my chest with sticky tape.

I could only see the girl by craning my head awkwardly. I definitely wanted a better view of her, so I turned on my side. I felt one of the sticky tapes on my chest come away and immediately the nice, reassuring *beep-bo* sound went *grrrr* as the dot of light passed out, the girl flung her paperback into the air, and rushed down the corridor shouting. 'MATRON, MATRON! HE'S GONE!'

Matron swept into the room, took in the situation at a glance, re-stuck the lost electrode to my chest, and the *beep-bo* routine came up again. The girl's face showed only happy relief. I pretended to be asleep to save her embarrassment.

'I see he's sleeping soundly,' Matron observed.

'Yes, Matron . . . Matron——'

'Yes?'

'He's Eric Morecambe of Morecambe and Wise.'

'Well, watch him. Show business. You can't be too careful.'

Before the next scene in my room, let me take you to Harpenden where on that night Joan had returned from a keep-fit class (she is an addict), had a bath, a snack and gone to bed. Gary was away in boarding school, at Aldenham, in Hertfordshire, and Gail was in bed upstairs.

The telephone rang and a Northern voice told Joan that her husband had been admitted to Leeds Royal Infirmary. She did not quite take it in because when we had spoken on the phone the evening before it seemed to her I was my normal self except for a slight rheumatism in the arm.

The Northern voice suggested she rang the Infirmary in about an hour's time when, the voice added, 'we ought to have more news for you'. He gave her the number and put the receiver down.

At first Joan thought someone was playing a nasty, practical joke. She immediately telephoned the Leeds number to check. Yes, it was the Infirmary. Yes, her husband had been admitted and was in a private room.

She came downstairs, made herself a cup of coffee, waiting for the hour to elapse to ring again. After an eternity for Joan, the time came. She got through to the night sister.

'The doctor is still with your husband. He has had a coronary. We won't have any news for a little while, but if you'd like try again in half an hour.'

Joan phoned her brother Alan in Finchley. He had been working very late at a dinner-dance at his hotel. 'I'll come over straight away,' he said.

Before Alan arrived, Joan heard from the night sister. 'He's comfortable now, but we would like you to come up to Leeds as soon as possible.'

'How urgent is it?' Joan asked. 'Do you want me to leave immediately?'

'The sooner the better,' she said.

Joan's problem was that she had a 15-year-old daughter asleep upstairs. She didn't want to alarm Gail, and leave her alone for the rest of the night in a state of fear about her father's condition.

When Alan arrived, it was late enough to start packing and for the gardener who lives nearby to be called. His wife would see to the child. Then Gail woke with all the bustle going on, and took the news well. Joan and Alan could now leave. It was after six.

Just before getting into the car, Joan said, 'I'll ring the hospital again.'

She did, but it was a different sister now who said, 'Haven't you left yet?'

'No, but it's a fairly straight run up the M1.'

'Well', the sister said, 'I hope you'll be here in time.'

Imagine Joan's state on that 160-mile drive to Leeds. They did it in record time, and were met by the sister who had phoned.

'Oh Mrs Morecambe, I hope I didn't alarm you but when we spoke on the phone I really thought your husband was breathing his last. I'm glad to say he's improved a bit. But please don't excite him. Just be very calm.'

I looked up at Joan through the plastic, her face swollen and her beautiful eyes puffed up with crying. She waved to me. Then the sister came in and she was led out of the room.

Outside in the corridor, the specialist attending me said, 'Mrs Morecambe, your husband has been told he has had a *slight* heart attack. The truth is he has had a serious heart attack. For the moment he is to see literally nobody except you, and even you are to limit your visits to very short periods because these next three days will be critical. You may sit with him for a while but stay in one corner and quietly knit or read but do not even speak to him.'

The result was that I did not see any other visitors except Ernie and Doreen for a few minutes. It was hard on Ernie. On the night of the attack he had received a phone call in his hotel shortly after he and Doreen had gone to bed. It was from the Leeds Royal Infirmary, from a sister with a very Yorkshire voice, who said Eric was in hospital. Ernie immediately thought it was an accident. She said no, a heart attack.

Next morning Ernie and Doreen came to see me. Joan was outside my room with the sister on duty when they arrived. At that moment the Matron walked up.

'How is he?' Ernie asked with what we call his 'lovable' smile.

The Matron's reply was so blunt Ernie went white. Ernie is all heart. I can guess how he must have felt, yet when he and Doreen came into my room all he said was, 'You'll do anything for a laugh.'

'Didn't you bring any grapes?'

'We don't grow them in Yorkshire.'

'You don't even *buy* them in Yorkshire.'

'Anyhow,' he said, 'here's a bunch of flowers. I got them at half-price.'

'Put them in water and they'll do for the wreath!'

Ernie didn't even wince but Joan told me long afterwards that he was in tears when he came out of the room.

He phoned my mother, but couldn't speak, he was so upset. He then went to my hotel room in Selby to collect my things and pay the bill. That upset him too when it came to packing personal things of mine like shoes and my joke books, and he went outside, our mild, gentle Ernie and roundly told off the hotel porter because he couldn't get his car out of the car park.

ERNIE We took Eric's things back to Joan's hotel in Leeds, then went out to Batley to see Jimmy Corrigan. Jimmy was dazed.

His first reaction was to close the club for the rest of the week and give people their money back—he's like that; he was just as upset as I was.

'The show must go on,' I said. 'I'm sure you can book another act if you get on the phone.' I mentioned a comic who happened to be in Leeds at the time.

Jimmy picked up the phone on his desk and got straight through to the comic. Jimmy explained the position.

'Will you stand in for Morecambe and Wise?' he asked.

'I'll do it for £1,000 a night,' the comic said. The voice on the phone was loud enough for me to hear.

Jimmy's face went red. Veins bulged on his forehead. He said, 'I'll pay £1000 a night for your services—to your favourite charity.'

'Nothing doing,' said the comic. 'I'm my own favourite charity.'

Jimmy banged down the receiver. Later, Jimmy was able to book another comic and Joan Turner and they stood in for us for the two nights that remained of the week.

Doreen and I went to see my mother—she has a flat in Leeds. She was in tears. She loves Eric, but she couldn't help expressing a thought which I suppose is only natural for any mother—'I'm glad it wasn't you.'

The next problem to be coped with was the press. The phone hadn't stopped ringing. I got through to our agent, Billy Marsh. We discussed a statement based on the advice of the specialist attending Eric, who insisted that nothing should be printed that might possibly reach Eric and cause alarm.

It was to the effect that the patient had suffered 'a slight coronary thrombosis and was progressing satisfactorily'.

The intensive care team watching Eric had noted that the moment he saw anybody he knew, especially in show business, his electrocardiograph went mad. He is built that way. A couple of press people invaded the room and began taking photographs. That had an even worse effect. It meant he had to be kept under constant watch. Over two hundred telegrams had arrived for him and there were sacks of letters besides phone calls every day from myself and scores of friends—a big strain on the hospital administration to whom we remain eternally grateful for the wonderful way in which they coped.

Eric was shown none of these, though Joan read them all and replied herself to a vast number of them. There were holy medals—one, a Lourdes medal, Eric still wears on his watch-strap. It was extremely touching to think that Eric was so generally loved. Naturally, all the letters and telegrams could not be answered personally, so notices of thanks for kind wishes were inserted in personal columns of newspapers.

After three weeks in hospital, Eric was allowed to go home. The TV room on the ground floor of the house was fitted out as a kind of bed-sitter so that he did not have to use the stairs. A diet sheet was drawn up to bring his weight down with full instructions regarding his treatment which included NO visitors, NO excitement, and everything else to be kept on a quiet, even level.

A car arrived at the hospital. It was to pick up Eric and Joan and take them to Harpenden.

'Time to get dressed. Come, let's get you out of bed,' said the nurse.

Eric had been on his feet before—his specialist believed in getting heart patients up and about as soon as possible. All of a sudden Eric's morale collapsed. Here in the womb of the hospital with everything at hand to preserve him, he felt secure. Now he was about to go into the outside world where there would be no oxygen tents or specialists immediately on tap. He suddenly felt sick and frightened. He began climbing back into bed.

'Send the car away,' he told Joan. 'I'm not fit, I'm not fit. I want to stay here.'

It took quite a bit of gentle persuasion to get him back on his feet.

Doreen and I saw him shortly after his return home. He looked as he had felt the day he had left hospital—old and sick. However, gradually, with everything revolving around his recovery, he began to enjoy all the fuss, his breakfast in bed, reading the newspapers from cover to cover, taking things easy, pottering about.

It was a slow, steady progress but with the whole burden of work unfortunately on Joan whose daily help had left and she hadn't been able as yet to engage her successor.

The question of visitors remained a problem. So many people wanted to see Eric. One day his old friend Terry Hall rang. Could he and his wife Kathy come to cheer him up?

Joan thought, Eric's bored. It shouldn't do any harm, having them come over for a little while.

'Yes,' she told Terry.

They arrived. Eric greeted them with, 'Who goes there, friend or enema?'

Eric was thrilled, and at once began telling them the saga of the heart-attack, re-enacting the part with all the trimmings.

In the middle of his story he suddenly went pale, clutched his heart and flopped down on the settee.

'Send for the doctor, send for the doctor. I don't feel too good.' To Terry, 'You'd better go.'

Poor Terry and Kathy, they felt awful. As it happened, it wasn't another attack; it was just that until Eric was fully recovered he was likely to feel a bit weak whenever he got too excited and energetic. In short, he was going to have to learn to live with his heart condition.

'How long am I going to stay like this?' Eric asked.

'Well,' said the doctor, 'the average case is off work for about three months.'

Eric said, 'In my line of business it's impossible to work without tension. You need tension to make a show come alive. So I'll stay off work for six months.'

Gentle walks were prescribed, not too far but preferably in the country. Just walking proved a bit of a bore, so Eric bought a little book on British birds and got out an old pair of binoculars, and that started his present bird-watching craze.

Then one day the front door bell rang. It was the doctor. Eric went pale.

'What do you want?' Eric said. 'Did Joan phone you?'

'No.'

'You haven't come to collect your bill?'

'No.'

'That's a relief. Couldn't we pay you in kind? A few sacks of potatoes?'

'Here, catch.' The doctor threw Eric his car keys. 'You're going to drive me down to the Watford driving range, and we're going to start practising your swing.'

Eric clutched his heart. 'B-but . . .'

'Look, it's a couple of months since the attack. You can do it, and I'll be with you.'

So Eric was led outside like a lamb to the slaughter. He drove the car, so slowly and nervously it was like a funeral cortege until the line of impatient cars he was holding up were able to pass him with a chorus of raspberry toots.

Eric started driving golf balls, looking round every few minutes for his doctor to tell him he had had enough.

'Carry on,' said the doctor, 'you're doing fine, but a little more power, more lift to the ball.'

Eventually Eric was allowed to stop, but it was the perfect psychological jerk he needed. He was no longer thinking like an invalid. Next stop show business.

He rang me up bubbling with enthusiasm. It was wonderful listening to him. This was the old Eric.

'We have only one problem,' I said.

'What's that?'

'Our writers,' I said.

Shortly after the heart attack I had received a phone call from the *Daily Express*.

'Is it true that your script writers, Hills and Green, have signed a contract with ATV?' the caller asked.

'I can't answer that because I honestly don't know,' I replied.

I did not give the matter much further thought. One often has calls like that from the press.

A week later, Doreen and I were in New York where I was

trying to sell repeats of our shows to Ed Sullivan. We then thought we'd fly down to Barbados for a holiday. On the plane the chief steward came up to me and said, 'I see you have lost your writers.'

I looked at him in amazement. 'I know nothing about this.'

'Well,' he said, 'I saw it in the papers.'

From Barbados I wrote to Doreen's father to make enquiries. He phoned Dick Hills, and only then did I get confirmation, in a letter from Hills, that they had in fact signed a contract to write exclusively for ATV and could no longer write for us.

In fairness I feel the situation needs a brief explanation. It seemed that it came out, when our return to television was being considered, that the services of Hills and Green were no longer available to us. Billy Marsh, our agent, then discussed with their agent, Roger Hancock, how the news should be broken to us. It was decided between them that Sid and Dick were the ones to tell Eric and Ernie. It was only human that this unhappy chore should have been put on the 'long finger' as they say. Unhappily nothing was done about it. We blame no one. It's just the way things sometimes happen.

16

ERNIE Our comeback to show business was unhurried, and being laid off work had certain compensations. For the first time in our lives we realised what a wonderful time people outside show business had at Christmas. We were able to eat, drink and make merry with the thought, so foreign to us, that we could really relax. *Relax* in a wonderful stupor of good food and booze without any worries about being on the job the next day. Our appearance on the Christmas Day show, *Night With The Stars*, had been recorded some weeks before the heart attack, as had our Morecambe and Wise show on Boxing Day.

Both went down very well, to judge from the reviews. Telegrams and good wishes for Eric's speedy recovery and our return to the box poured in.

I mokeyed around, occasionally phoning Eric and doing a bit of PR for Morecambe and Wise. I talked about Eric at ladies' luncheon clubs. I guest-starred at schools and Girl Guide concerts. I gave press interviews. I got some of our Morecambe and Wise shows repeated on TV. I appeared on the Eamonn Andrews show. I published *The Morecambe and Wise Joke Book*. I did a few radio programmes like *Housewives' Choice*. I always mentioned Eric, and one day as a surprise I was able to say, 'And, ladies, here is Eric Morecambe in person, by kind permission of his doctor!' He had been allowed out that day to say a few words on the air. All this brought in a small income that I split with Eric.

ERIC I'll say this for Ern, he split everything right down the middle, including my share!

ERNIE It wasn't an easy position for me to be in. I couldn't very well go out and start doing things on my own—not that I wanted to—until something definite was settled about Eric's future. If in the end the doctor said he could never work again, that would put a completely different complexion on it. In the meantime I had to stand by him, as I am sure he would have done me.

His progress was slow—he had had such a fright, though there was comfort for him from the fact that Bernie Delfont, who had had a heart attack fifteen years before, was still on the job, making money and smoking eight cigars a day. There was Sid James, another member of the 'coronary club'; Eric was delighted when he saw Sid back on the box. There was Reg Varney, and of course Peter (Lazarus) Sellers, to name but a few.

By May the situation had begun to resolve itself. Eric was definitely going to work again. His improvement continued, then at last in August 1969 we did a show together again at the Winter Garden Theatre in Bournemouth. It was a Sunday concert. We were introduced by Frankie Vaughan and got a standing ovation of over four minutes—pure Hollywood that brought out a few handkerchiefs in the audience, and on the stage.

We still had four shows to do for the BBC on an existing contract. Billy Cotton Jr, head of Light Entertainment for BBC-TV, could have opted out on the grounds that Eric wasn't fit enough for the risks involved. But Billy had said, 'No, I want you boys to do these shows, and I am prepared to wait.' This was when Eric was still fairly ill.

Not only that. In July, Bill, in yet a further demonstration of his faith in us, signed another contract for us to continue to do thirteen shows a year for the BBC over the next three years, each show to take three weeks in rehearsal and two days in actual shooting in the studio, a precedent unheard of in comedy. The idea being that Eric should not be put under excessive strain.

The problem of a script was also solved by Bill. 'There's Eddie Braben,' he said. 'He's been writing for Ken Dodd for years, but no longer.'

'We've heard some very funny lines out of Ken Dodd. If they're from Eddie Braben, Eddie would do very nicely for us,' we said.

'Let's get Eddie to write you a show,' said Bill.

We met Eddie Braben at the BBC-TV Centre in Shepherds Bush. Bill was there.

Eddie was tall, about thirty-eight, and pure Liverpool, which we promised we wouldn't hold against him. He had been a barrow boy in St John's Market, in the centre of Liverpool, and used to give his customers so much lip and gags that one customer, who could understand the lingo (I believe it has an affinity with Swahili), suggested he should write for comics. Eddie had to start from scratch—learn the alphabet. Eventually he sold a page of jokes to a comic for five shillings. He was making fifteen shillings a week out of his market-stall jokes when he met Ken Dodd and became his staff gag-writer, a job he kept for twelve years.

Eddie was honest with us. He said, 'Really, I'm only a gag man. I have never done situations and sketches.'

'We appreciate that,' Bill said. 'I'll tell you what, we'll suggest a few ideas and situations, and you go away and write the boys a show. How's that?'

Eddie went away with a few ideas on the back of an envelope. What he came up with, subject to some suggestions and modifications from ourselves and Johnny Ammonds, our producer, became the basis of the first of our new shows. It was well received. We let Eddie write another three shows before he became our official writer. We were on to a new formula which I feel has kept getting better.

Our method of working remained very much as it had been with Hills and Green, except that Eddie provides us with more than just a sheet of ideas. Eddie sends us a completely scripted show on which Eric and I will do some further work with the gags and situations. It is a happy collaboration.

Since Eddie's advent my stage character has subtly changed— I am now put over as quite a mixture of meanness, ego and vanity, and it has come over very well, with the familiar gags about my wig—'You can't see the join'—and my 'short, fat, hairy legs'. I should add that a great deal of credit for ideas and gags and, most important of all, putting them across, is due to Johnny Ammonds, whom we first met when he succeeded Ronnie Taylor as our producer of *Variety Fanfare* in Manchester nearly twenty years ago.

Johnny made his name as a TV producer in the original Harry Worth and Val Doonican shows. It is to Johnny and indeed his whole team that our special thanks are due for helping us to win our awards, in 1970, 1971 and 1972, for the Best Light Entertainment Performance on TV.

As for our health, it is I, not Eric, who has ever given Johnny cause for anxiety. This was when we were doing the Christmas show in 1969 and I went down with 'flu. Luckily Johnny already had sufficient material in the can to put something together.

Since then I have always had an anti-flu injection every winter, though I'm beginning to feel I would rather have the 'flu than the antidote!—rather like the remark of a very acid critic, after seeing a certain comic's TV show, 'Isn't it time he changed places with his warm-up man? The *before* was much funnier than the *during*.'

Warm-up men are the fellows who are sent out before the show to de-glum a studio audience. We've warned our warm-up men, John Junkin, Barry Cryer and Alan Curtis to watch it. The first time a similar remark is made about us, they're out!

Outside of TV we have two interests. One is our stage act. We still do an hour and a quarter and in that time you will see over thirty years of Morecambe and Wise pass before your very eyes. We accept perhaps twenty-five of these engagements a year—Eric calls it doing a bank raid. But money apart, it keeps us in touch with live audiences who have paid for their seats. It means too that if all else fails we still have our act.

Pantomimes and summer seasons? You may well ask. The answer lies in what this book is all about. In other words, why should we get back into the treadmill when we don't need the extra money and in any case we would kill ourselves before we could enjoy it? Besides, we are keen to have another bash at a film.

Films are the only door to the international market, though I don't think I shall ever be entirely happy in the medium until they can perfect the use of several cameras used simultaneously in extended takes. Short takes do not suit our style. We can't spark off each other when one of us says something and the other may have to wait twenty or thirty minutes before he can reply. Anyhow, there are plans ahead for two big films, and this time they'll be good.

ERIC I feel that fundamentally we have come to terms with ourselves on what we want to do and what we want out of life. Our priorities are different now, but it took a real jolt to make us realise we were missing out on so much. For me, for one thing, there was that important matter of getting to know my own children, taking an interest in their lives and interests, and not having that dead look in your eyes when they start telling you about their school or friends. This may sound odd to the average father, but the truth is Ernie and I had become compulsives about work and show business to the virtual exclusion of all else. Life had become remote like the sound of traffic through a closed hotel window. People were faces in a darkened auditorium. Money was just figures on a piece of paper and the thought of further tax demands. It didn't mean enjoying the sunshine with your wife or taking that drawn, worried look off her face. It didn't mean using your senses to feel the very *texture* of our God-given gifts, the colours of autumn, the sparkle of morning dew, the scents of the country. It didn't mean I could take an interest in any subject for its own sake, like Joan does, in antiques, to learn to look at them with the eye of an expert, to *explore* their beauty.

My great mistake, until I was lucky enough to be shown the error of my ways, was in always being in too much of a hurry. My mother's name for me was perfect—Jifflearse. All I wanted was to take in as much as I could in as short a time as possible. Now that's all right for a growing lad. He needs a quick, wide picture of everything that's going on around him. Later he can fill in the details and enjoy observing them, and thanks to the way things have turned out I have been able to grow up.

Naturally Ernie has experienced the change of pace in a different way. Now he can go to some function to which we are invited, as we were recently to the Lord Mayor's Banquet, and really enjoy the pomp and panoply without its being marred by the thought of the money we'd be losing by not working that night.

Surprisingly enough, Ernie does actually spend money on a good time—taking Doreen out to dinner, at the White Elephant, in Curzon Street, the club used a lot by film people, the Twenty-One Club, the Trattoria Terrazza, in Romilly Street, really expensive places.

He and Doreen have formed a supper club. They take it in turns every week to entertain, or be entertained by, the Billy Daintys, the Philip Joneses, the Vince Powells, the Harry Worths, Pearl Carr and Teddy Johnson. All of whom are in, or involved in, show business. They have drinks, a fork supper and a lovely time talking show biz and shredding showbiz characters.

For their holidays Ernie and Doreen go to Malta. They do a lot of touring in Europe, including Spain where Ernie will go into paroxysms of pleasure watching himself on TV speaking fluent Spanish and not understanding a word except 'si'.

He spends the week-ends in Peterborough counting the bricks in his house there and surveying the garden with quiet satisfaction, He likes swimming, provided his knees are covered. He plays cricket in occasional, PRO-promoted charity matches for the Lords Taverners (don't ask me what it means), and has had the distinction of scoring several ducks against bowling so devastating that the bowler has had to be pointed in the direction of the batsman and given a push.

I once tried to initiate him into the mysteries of football when his home-town team, Peterborough United, invited him to become a director of their club. We went to a home match against Oldham. During the play I tried to explain what the game was all about. Peterborough won and everyone around us was cheering. Ernie included.

'I'm going to congratulate *our* boys,' he told me. He led me into a dressing-room.

'Great game,' he said.

'No, it wasn't,' they said.

'Yes, it was,' said Ernie.

'No, it wasn't. How could it be?'

'You won. What more do you want?' Ernie demanded.

'No, we lost.'

Ernie was in the wrong dressing-room. Our exit from the club was unobtrusive.

Another esoteric pastime of Ernie's is his motor-cruiser. Ernie sold that boat to Bill Cotton Jr—at a profit—because he saw something bigger and fatter at the Boat Show with an extra cabin and a shower. A motor-cruiser on the Broads is Ernie's idea of getting away from it all.

Joan and I lead a rather different life. From the start we made up our minds that our home lives would be as near to average as it was humanly possible, first so that our children could grow up in an environment and against a background that had nothing of the gloss and artificiality of show business, and secondly so that we ourselves would remain 'safe'—I think that's the word—from its more insidious dangers. It may make us sound a bit dull, but we have become a part of a little circle of friends in Harpenden who have nothing to do with show business and do not attribute any of our odd and peculiar ways to our being in show business and therefore 'different'.

This is not to say we don't give and go to show business parties which are always marvellous fun. The last we went to was given by Mike and Bernie Winters about ten weeks ago. We left early, at about eight in the morning. My guess is that it's still on.

The reports on our children must remain 'fluid'. At the time of going to press, Gail, who went to Winkfield and did a Cordon Bleu course in cookery, then decided she wanted to do nursery nursing. She is being trained in this at Walgarth, a college at Golders Green, and has become proficient at all the correct nappy-changing drills. She is twenty. Gary, two and a half years younger, is still at Aldenham. He has ambitions to be a writer.

My parents are thriving, I'm glad to say. Not long ago we sent them on a trip to America. They went by sea and toured the continent by Greyhound coach. They had the adventure of their lives, got involved with Texan millionaires, were invited to weddings and went up in a helicopter.

When we met them on their return, my mother said, 'It was wonderful but it's more wonderful being home. All I want now is to see that sunset again, over Morecambe Bay.'

'And you, Dad?' I asked.

'I want to get on the other side of a pint of good English beer.'

'There was a time when we thought he was teetotal,' I said.

'Don't mind him,' my mother said. 'That was what he told the education authority to get a licence for you to do that party piece of yours in the clubs. What was it?'

'*I'm Not All There,*' I said.

'Come to think of it, you never were!' she said. 'How's Ernie?'

He and Doreen were seen at that moment pushing their way through the crowds at the station. Everybody greeted everybody else.

'How's Connie?' my mother asked.

Ernie said his mother was fine and was shortly leaving for Australia to spend a while with his sister Constance.

And so, after we had all had a drink, we wended our separate ways homeward. Everything, thank God, was right with the world. Ernie will tell you that. He goes through life with a seraphic smile, happy and patient every morning of his life, even when he's got a hangover. It drives his wife mad. He spends ages in his bath, shaving, having happy thoughts about his bank balance. Then there's his coffee making—he even roasts the beans, so after all that you've got to squeeze your mouth into a sort of a wry expression of liking something like medicine, and smile and say it's lovely.

Doreen is very energetic and efficient. Their houses are like new pins. Doreen will go into bouts of spring cleaning and throw out old clothes Ernie has been hoarding for years—he can't bear to part with anything. Yet all he will say is, 'You're busy, shall I get the lunch?'

ERNIE I've let him have his little fun. Now I'll tell you about our Eric. He is supposed to be a bird-watcher, but he is terrified of anything with a beak. Once years ago his father trained a robin to come down and take bird-seed off his hand. Eric was a large nipper at the time. Must have been about ten. One day his dad put bird-seed on his son's hand, who held it out for the little robin. Eric was so paralysed with fear that the bird-seed was shaken off his hand. That's Eric, and he hasn't changed. He's a hobbies man. He collects things. At the moment it's clocks and pictures, but he'll soon get bored with them as he does with whatever fad he's chasing.

Only a woman like Joan could live with him. There she is in the kitchen with her cat and two dogs and her papers and correspondence spread out on the kitchen table, coping with his tax. She is the gentle dynamo that powers Eric Morecambe. It's even got to the stage that when they go out together to a function, and a plate of food is put in front of Eric, he will turn to his wife and say, 'Do I like this?' You can imagine the ordeal it has been for *me*, working with him.

ERIC   OK, that's enough. All the reader now wants to know is about the future. Look at the Referee. He's got the whistle in his mouth. We're well into injury time, so wrap it up.

ERNIE   Wrap what up?

ERIC   The book, stupid. Now about the future. Of course, my big worry is what I'm going to do when one of us dies.

ERNIE   Yes, and who gets the custody of the joke books?

ERIC   You wanted the last word.

ERNIE   It's something I've never said before in the thirty-odd (very odd) years we've been together. It's a wish I've nursed in my heart.

ERIC   Speak it.

ERNIE   It's just that I'd like to borrow your bald wig. I want to see what I'll look like in another thirty years.

ERIC   Let's swop shirts?

ERNIE   Referee!!!!!!!!

ERIC   That was eight. I counted them.

ERNIE   I demand my last word.

ERIC   All right. What's it to be?

ERNIE   Wait for it . . . Folks, my last word and testament is— CRINKLE.

Whistle

ERIC PS: Luton for the Cup!

WHISTLE